A Place to Land

Also by Martha Manning

Undercurrents:
A Life Beneath the Surface

Chasing Grace:
Reflections of a Catholic Girl, Grown Up

Restoring Intimacy:
A Patient's Guide to Maintaining Relationships
During Depression (co-author)

All Seasons Pass:
Grieving a Miscarriage

The Common Thread:
Mothers and Daughters:
The Bond We Never Outgrow

A Place to Land

Lost and Found
in an Unlikely Friendship

MARTHA MANNING

BALLANTINE BOOKS • NEW YORK

Many of the names in this story have been changed
to protect the privacy of individuals who appear in these pages.

A Ballantine Book
Published by The Random House Publishing Group

Copyright © 2003 by Martha Manning

All rights reserved under International and
Pan-American Copyright Conventions. Published in the
United States by The Random House Publishing Group,
a division of Random House, Inc., New York,
and simultaneously in Canada by
Random House of Canada Limited, Toronto.

Ballantine and colophon are registered
trademarks of Random House, Inc.

www.ballantinebooks.com

Library of Congress Cataloging-in-Publication Data can be obtained
from the publisher upon request.

ISBN 0-345-45055-8

Design by Julie Schroeder

Manufactured in the United States of America

First Edition: July 2003

2 4 6 8 10 9 7 5 3 1

for Raina

Wild Geese

You do not have to be good.
You do not have to walk on your knees
for a hundred miles through the desert, repenting.
You only have to let the soft animal of your body
       loves what it loves.
Tell me about despair, yours, and I will tell you mine.
Meanwhile the world goes on.
Meanwhile the sun and the clear pebbles of the rain
are moving across landscapes,
over the prairies and the deep trees,
the mountains and rivers.
Meanwhile the wild geese, high in the clean blue air,
are heading home again.
Whoever you are, no matter how lonely,
the world offers itself to your imagination,
calls to you like the wild geese, harsh and exciting —
over and over announcing your place
in the family of things.

— Mary Oliver

A Place to Land

Foreword

We sit on the sidelines watching as Deven's twin brother, Darren, and twenty other four- and five-year-olds learn the seemingly impossible integration of running, kicking, and watching where they're going—with the added goal of maintaining contact with the ball. The icing on the cake is when they learn to actually move the ball in the right direction. Fortunately, the laid-back coach of this team dispensed his own basic tenets of competitive sports for preschoolers:

Neither direction is the "right" direction.

Winning is a state of mind. We don't keep score.

You can almost feel the silent gnashing of teeth, the energy required for self-control, the instructions stifled in the throats of frustrated parents on the sidelines. Parents who agree, in spirit, with the coach but who also can't bear to see their little darlings score an exuberant point—in the other team's goal.

Deven uses my lap like I'm the human equivalent of a La-Z-Boy recliner. With each position I am expected to respond in kind, which gets a bit uncomfortable when he decides he wants to stretch out. Fifteen minutes into practice he is always hungry, thirsty, or bored. Today, his usual level of frustration is inching up because of the five-pound pack slung over his shoulder. At a quick glance, it could easily be mistaken for a sports bag or a backpack, but two seconds more focuses attention on the long, clear tubes and the humming, whirring, and beeping noises; and it becomes clear that this is not the burden of an ordinary five-year-old. This noisy, clumsy pack allows him the luxury of having chemotherapy delivered on an outpatient basis, instead of his usual, difficult hospitalizations.

It is his get-out-of-hospital pass—though it's never free. For a sensitive child, Deven is remarkably patient about using it. But at age five, he looks only three, and the large pack overwhelms all twenty-nine pounds of him. Each time he wants to get up to kick his own soccer ball on the sidelines, he runs a bit and then gets yanked back by the machine he's left beside me. He scowls as if I am responsible. On my energetic days I carry it alongside of him and run, but today it is growing dark and cold. I am tired and just want to sit. I've already bribed him with the promise of ice cream after practice and pray the Good Humor truck shows up, because Deven's displeasure has, since infancy, been routinely difficult to take.

Over the past two years of his illness, he has progressed beyond using only his body to express his feelings, fight his battles, and connect him to the people he loves. Words were never a currency in which he traded easily. Better a quick kiss or a hang-on-tight hug than "I'm happy" or "I'm really liking you right now." Better a bite or a scratch or a slicing scream than the too-simple words "I'm angry or frustrated or scared." Today he is sad, mad, and bored—the triple threat. I suspect from the dark-brown circles under his eyes and the grayish tint of his skin that he's also tired. But fatigue is something he never concedes, even as his eyes are in the process of closing for daily business and he's beginning to snore standing up.

He plops back down into my crossed legs and pulls my arms around him like a blanket. I spot a plane flying low enough on its descent into National Airport to make it potentially interesting to a restless little boy.

"Look, Deven, at the sky! . . . Look at that plane!" I point with exaggerated enthusiasm.

There are moments that pass through our lives, or that we pass through, the significance of which we are totally unaware of at the time. We usually know the big ones. We can even predict them—the events that go on family trees, invitations, and diplomas—signified by cakes and rings and letters of remembrance. We know the stuff of photographs—those moments we or someone else deem important enough to preserve. And many of those moments do alter our lives. They set and confirm us upon paths that are fairly well expected, even if the exact details are unclear.

There are other moments when the marked path vanishes entirely. There are blips, glitches, or outright reversals. We find ourselves creeping or crashing into branches or trees, tumbling over precipices we could never have anticipated. It is only in retrospect—way back in retrospect—that we see the convergence of events, the confluences of chance occurrences, the seemingly low-valence choices we made, ignorant of their import, or the choices others made on our behalf. Looking back, we can curse or praise these moments, these open spaces in which seeds we never anticipated planting took root and grew and grew and grew.

As Deven lifts his head, a formation of at least one hundred birds flies overhead. Their motion and noise intensify their sharp contrast against a sky that is slowly giving up its late autumn evening pinks, purples, and oranges. Suddenly the jet recedes in importance. He leaps up and points to the birds, demanding, "Look at them! What are they doing?"

"They're going away," I tell him.

"Why?" he asks in a tone that lets me know that no simple answer will suffice.

"Well, it's getting colder and winter's coming soon. The cold is hard on the birds. They can't find food."

"But where do they go?" Deven persists.

"To a warmer place," I explain, "someplace south."

"Like to somebody's big house?" he asks.

"No, not really. Birds weren't made for people houses. Remember when you made that wish last winter and you got to go to Disney World, and it was really cold when you left your apartment, but then when you got to Florida it was sunny and warm?"

"Yeah, we didn't need no coats no more."

"Well, that's the kind of place they go."

"Disney World?" he asks, his face so screwed up in puzzlement that I have to fight not to laugh.

"No, not Disney World exactly but to places that are warm like Disney World where you never need to wear a coat."

"Or a stupid hat?" he asks, scowling as he tugs off his baseball hat and throws it on the ground. I try to avoid the inevitable power struggle that is just waiting for my command to put the hat back on his head.

"Hey," I say, grabbing his little hat from the dirt and placing it on my big head, "I wonder what a bird would look like in a baseball hat."

"Better than you, stupid head," he replies. He grabs his hat and puts it back where it belongs. In exchange for his acceding to my unspoken authority, I let the "stupid head" remark—a particular favorite of his—pass.

"Do they have to go away forever?" he asks with concern.

"No, that's the cool part," I explain. "Every spring they come back."

"How do they get their selves home?" he asks with concern. "How do they know the place to land?"

As his questions deepen, my knowledge heads toward the shallow end.

"Um," I stumble, "they remember and they look at nature to tell them where they should go."

"Do their moms know?" Deven whispers.

"Oh yeah," I answer.

We talk about how people move, like how he'll be moving into a brand-new house with his whole family.

"Do the babies stay with their mothers?" he interrupts.

"Oh, of course they do," I assure him.

"But what if the moms are flying real fast and the babies get lost? . . . The babies don't know the way, just the moms? . . . What happens then?"

The mounting anxiety in his voice signals that this conversation is veering much more in the direction of human mothers and their babies than their avian counterparts. I feel him shiver against my chest, and he doesn't fight me when I bend to button his jacket. Every few seconds he burrows in for more warmth and comfort. But then I feel his body jolt with yet another concern, another unanswered question. I'm starting to wish he'd been more impressed with the plane. We're flying into far more dangerous territory now.

"What if they get lost?"

Babies and mommies are a big deal to this kid. During his long hospitalizations he has had to learn to tolerate so many separations from his mom, my friend Raina. Most nights his mother was able to get his brother and sister settled and then return to the hospital to sleep over. Deven would fight to stay awake until she came. And if she didn't come exactly on time, he'd get nurses to call his home or his aunties or me to register his panic, to see if we knew where his mom was or to just pass the time while he cried and we tried to find something that might distract him momentarily.

"My mommy said she was gonna come, but I don't know what time it is and she didn't come yet. . . . Do you know where my mommy is? . . . It's been dark for ten hours!" We'd hang out on the phone in these excruciating calls, reflections of his everyday struggle to manage being separated from the one person in his life who was his portable home. Wherever his mom was, even in a scary hospital room, was home for Deven. My constant reassurance that Mommy always comes is met with the litany of times she was late or unavoidably unable to make it. Deven's memory for disappointment is extraordinary.

I keep watch as his brother, Darren, steps out to the ball. He kicks the hell out of it, is thrilled with himself, and holds up both arms in a salute of success, which I return. He's so thrilled with himself that the coach has to remind him that kicking is usually followed by running. Then it's back to Deven.

"You know," I tell him, "I'm really sure that the mommy bird and the babies stay together the whole time. They leave together, they fly together, they find a warm home together, and then they come back here together . . . every springtime."

Another organized, purposeful flank of birds, backlit by the fading sun, stands out sharply against the darkening sky. Deven leaps up and, with a total lack of self-consciousness, waves and yells, "Hey, you birds. Bye! Have a good vacation! Stay with your mom, okay? Come back when it's warm, okay? See you in the spring!" —all at the top of his lungs.

He sings out to them in the full certainty that he and the birds are actually communicating—one of those wonderful suspensions of boundaries between children and the rest of the natural world. I get a huge charge out of the absolute spontaneity of preschoolers. It kicks in with a deep, unashamed laugh reserved only for children. Deven is annoyed that I am not doing my part in the bon voyage and coaches me in what to say. Then he freely corrects me when I'm not loud or enthusiastic enough.

As the birds cross the sky, we sing in concert, "Bye! See you next spring! Bye!" As I watch him wave, I register a solid punch to my solar plexus. "Next spring . . . See you in the spring." Then comes the ache of knowing that despite the exuberance of his farewells and his enthusiasm for the future that by sheer medical probabilities the birds have a far greater likelihood of greeting the spring than does the little boy waving beside me.

A Dividend of Darkness

I have spent much of the past few years battling depression. When I emerge from one of those relentless, frightening periods, I try to construct some sense of what I've taken from the experience—what I've learned and how I've changed. But I never come up with much, except an increasing terror that I might fall again.

One of the dividends of long exposures to the darkness is a greater sensitivity to the light. To find yourself caught in relentless shadows that are not subject to day or hour, to effort, or to help or even to love or prayer—just the passage of an indeterminate amount of time—is to plunge to a level of excruciating helplessness. Our lives are illuminated in so many ways, only a fraction by our own effort and design. When the light fades, any built-in ability to deregulate, to make due with less, to automatically sharpen our sensibilities is impaired by our dependence upon the cheap light all around us. A few of us know what it is like to exist against our will in a gray fog so bleak it's impossible to see our own hands in front of us.

We are reminded that we know the world much less well than we thought. It's humbling and bruising to exist in this darkness. There are so many ways that shadows lengthen and loom, threaten to cover the difference between day and night. To be stuck in the dark puts us on notice—for the fragility of our safety and survival. Our world narrows to the simple environs we can move around in, to people who depend on us or who we depend upon for care. The world constricts, and self-preservation is the only name of the game.

Depression is one such darkness. It is all the more frustrating because this personal disaster is internally driven or, in other words, always feels like "my own fault." I have written about depression. How it slowly sucks the air from all the well-being in any room. How your strongest desire is to escape. Until you realize any room will become a tomb within minutes of your entry. One tiny corner of your mind yells out, "This will end. It will end like before." But the rest of you can't see things coming out well.

And then, you're always totally surprised and grateful as hell when they do.

Few of us are gifted with an innocent and universal compassion. We have to stub our own toes, crash our own cars, hurt ourselves or those we love. Then we come to realize the infinite combinations and permutations of mistake, evil, rotten luck, or bad karma that the world dishes out. The plain horror at the multiplicity of ways that things can go bad. The minimal power that we, mere humans, often have to stop those bad things or, for that matter, to even see them coming.

By my mid-forties, it's finally become clear that, to me, there are perhaps only two things that generate profit from the currency of suffering—the slow accumulation of wisdom and compassion. But I'm beginning to think that, in this life, they're worth a lot.

MY GIRL

I hang up from a marathon call from my nineteen-year-old daughter, Keara. I'm still not entirely used to the absence of the slamming door in the late afternoon, with the exact same declaration, "I'm ho-ome," a song I've come to miss since she left for college in New York.

Keara is our only child. We had her in our mid-twenties, right after Brian started his first job as a clinical social worker making a big ten thousand dollars a year and I was enrolled in a demanding Ph.D. program in clinical psychology. People told me I was nuts. That I should wait till I was finished with school, internships, and fellowships before having children. But I believed firmly in the power of my own unlimited drive and energy and went ahead with my first child. Then in my mid-thirties, when I was "settled," I had two painful miscarriages. They were losses that rocked my belief that whatever I wanted in life was a matter of talent, effort, and good planning.

I had taken antidepressant medicines before both pregnancies, planning to discontinue them during each nine-month stretch. There was general agreement among a number of specialists that I remain on medicine during subsequent pregnancies. After a great deal of reflection I decided I could not live with any lowered odds of having a healthy baby due to medicine I took during pregnancy. Brian and I made peace with the fact that we were blessed with only one child. It's been a little harder since that only child has taken flight.

I love my daughter like crazy. Even when we push each other's buttons like nobody's business, even when she knows how to get to me like no one else. But what makes me miss her so much these days is that I like her so damn much. She's a voracious reader and an interesting thinker with a sense of humor like her father's; in her visits home we can sit at the dining room table or lie around on my bed and shoot the breeze for hours. She is my connection to the space between the present and the future. In our discussions about politics or film or feminism, I'll make a comment that sounds very smart to me, but then she looks at me like I'm one of the Beverly Hillbillies and I know I'm about to be humbled. She uses words like "deconstruct" as weapons against me, because after that, I'm always totally out of anything remotely intelligent to say.

Keara makes me uncomfortable in my self-satisfied liberal but hopelessly outdated mind-set. And, as much as I hate feeling like an intellectual fossil, when she leaves I find myself reading the books she's left behind. Of course, by the time I've digested them and "casually" bring them up in future conversations, she patiently explains to me what part of my reasoning is already yesterday's news.

Oh college. I'd love to go again. Just open up my mind, take subjects simply because they're interesting, with no nod to their utilitarian value. Not graduate school, not postdoctoral training. It took me years, singularly focused, to become a clinical psychologist. Then the teaching, researching, and practicing for many more years. In my late thirties I "accidentally" wrote a memoir that came from the journals of my first severe depression.

All of a sudden, my private love of writing expanded into more books, readings, and speaking engagements until I had a new career—absent all the planning and struggling of my younger years. My new career is far more public and far more private than my old one. I can go days without seeing anyone but my husband, Brian, simultaneously loving and hating the daily confrontation with the silent, blank computer screen. It is a good life, but one I never planned.

THE LITTLE FLYER THAT COULD

*C*hristmas mail makes me cranky. There are some simple cards that are treasures of the season. But more and more, I find it difficult to deal with the photos attached to letters on red or green paper detailing the lives of friends and acquaintances. They leave me envious or awestruck, depending on the day. Why do these letters distress me? Maybe it's that people are organized and energized enough to sit down, put together a written observance of their great lives, and have visual proof of it. Or maybe it's because they have an address book of people who *care*. To be honest, I suppose I'm jealous that they actually have lives that can fill two single-spaced pages.

I imagine doing my own for this year.

Seasons greetings,

I fell apart in January. It has been slow going ever since. But you probably know that already. Brian still stays with me, God knows why.

Keara lives in New York.
Happy holidays.

Let's face it. Not worth the stamp.

I've developed a hierarchy to determine which mail gets attention. The bills, possible checks, and letters written on personal stationery are keepers. The upscale catalogues rank high enough for their own temporary place in the bathroom library. Ever since I stopped being able to spend freely, I've developed a real appreciation of catalogues. Rather than depressing me, they bring me back to the land of wishing versus having. They bring me back to the hours my siblings and I pored over the Sears catalogue, bending down page corners, circling and initialing pictures and merchandise numbers very carefully, so that Santa would have no trouble differentiating between the Betsy Wetsy doll I so dearly wanted versus the boring Lincoln Logs my brother coveted so ferociously.

The envelopes in which there is clearly a "prize" in exchange for a donation always catch my attention, even though the gift is useless 99 percent of the time. Realtors and plumbers send refrigerator magnets. The Sisters of the Holy Rosary and compatriots usually offer address labels that I would never use because everywhere my name *isn't*, they've fit an image of some holy icon. The ones that make me feel really bad are those who send cheap medals with the image of a saint, adorned with a ribbon, presumably for pinning to my clothes. I don't know if it's superstition, but they live on—years' worth of them—safe in my top desk drawer. I can't bring myself to relegate a saint to the trash.

Then there are the plain community newsletters and brochures—black type on white paper, often folded and stapled in ways that travel badly, with absolutely nothing on the front that calls out *Forget about all that other trash. READ ME!* In our house these often take the most express route to oblivion.

The trip from sender to me is always an adventure, the majority of which occurs at my front door. There aren't many low-positioned door mail slots like mine on my mailman's route. Most are eye-level, roomy boxes next to people's doors. Or if he's really lucky, in the newer homes in the area, all he has to do is slide the stuff into a curbside, cavernous container so big you could store a bike in there.

When it comes to *my* house, however, he seems to take it personally when he can't fit the entire day's mail through the slot in one good push. On his laid-back days, he allows a few bills to slide in first. But, damn it, those satiny catalogues, those magazines, and the damn oversized manila envelopes—he is determined that those suckers go through *together*. The *condition* of the delivered material is low on his priority list. Last week, he must have had a huge load because he delivered the mail through the unyielding slot like he was giving birth. When I heard the commotion, I jumped out of my desk chair and sat at the top of the steps to listen. Let me tell you, they don't call it "delivering" the mail for nothing.

The Christmas cards and bills cascaded through without a hitch. He had stretched a rubber band around the catalogues with a white newsletter on the top. He got them a half inch in and pushed. Hard. I heard tearing. Finally in one huge battle of the bulge, they technically made it through. The editorial department of *The New Yorker* would not have been pleased with its treatment. The Saks, Nordstrom, and Macy's missives ended up slightly ripped, corners folded like accordions—none bad enough to disqualify them from bathroom placement.

An unadorned newsletter from the Arlington Homeless Shelter never made it to the floor. Ripped, with several staples undone, it hung precariously from the slot. As I pulled on it, it ripped even more, exposing a page having something to do with some sort of Santa program and homeless families that looked appealing. I don't know why, but I sat down amid all the mail and went directly for the newsletter. Two minutes reading left me immediately ashamed at how little I know about homelessness in my own community.

Having been so ill for almost a year, sure that my life would never again be any brighter than the ash gray I'd stumbled through for so long, I now know how fast and far it is possible for *anyone* to fall. Fall so hard that all of a sudden you need a bed, a job, a doctor, a source of hope—with no idea how to get it. These days I feel a whole lot closer to the people described in the newsletter than I do to the beauties on the front of the Saks catalogue or the super families in L.L. Bean ads.

The program in my community newsletter is a good one, but it comes up against my lack of confidence that I actually have the ability to "help" anyone else. In the Adopt-a-Family program, residents at a shelter write a wish list for themselves and their kids, and volunteers become "Santa" to that family by fulfilling some of their wishes. I read it over and over until a small voice opened the possibility: *I think I can . . . I think I can.* Of all the cards and the envelopes and the magazines and the ads that surrounded me on the floor of the front hall, it was the humble black-and-white ripped, stapled Arlington newsletter that gave this weary, doubting, shaky soul the sense that she was ready and the challenge to stop hiding behind the wrong side of the door.

CUTIE AND THE BEAST

I get a huge charge out of my nieces and nephews, especially the "littles," my sister Rachel's children. With an empty nest, I am so happy to have it filled, even if only occasionally. Tori, age four, is Rachel's oldest. Then there is sweet Gracie, a very young two, not yet ready to leave home. Little do they know, but a little boy will be joining the crowd in six months.

Tori and I bonded early on. She is a bright, imaginative child who reminds me of my daughter, Keara, at that age, except Tori is considerably more intense. She is a prize-winning architect when it comes to constructing mountains out of molehills. But she is also an affectionate pixie with a wonderfully throaty voice. After the birth of sister, Gracie, when Tori was two, I also identified with her travails and triumphs as she stepped into her big sister role.

Tori loves her sleep overs with Brian and me. And while I'd like to think it's because we're such wonderful people to be with, I suspect that it also is due to the fact that we spoil her rotten. When the Disney marketing group targets their conception of the perfect consumer, Tori's face comes on their screen. She loves it all—every character, every Disney detail.

Beauty and the Beast is the penultimate. I've seen the movie at least five times with her. I've sung the CD endlessly in the car. She is so tuned in to me that she can nail me whenever my mind wanders, even briefly—whether it's to add something to my mental grocery store list, to wonder what Keara's doing, or to mentally kick myself for painting such an ugly color on the bedroom walls. "Martha"—she elbows me gently or whispers loudly in my ear—"you're not paying attention." The good-news bad-news part of these videos is that you can buy and keep them with no limit to the amount of times she can watch them.

Tori's not a totally indiscriminate Disney fan. Anything frightening will lead to many missed hours of sleep and a parade of questions, concerns, and need for reassurance from my brother-in-law Greg or my sister. Greg has learned to preview any prospective video, and with the help of an extra video machine, he edits out the stuff of potential nightmares. It was two years, for example, before Tori was aware that *The Wizard of Oz* had *any* wicked witches. Over time it became a matter of adjusting the dosage of possibly offensive material, so that there are now at least five different versions of *The Wizard of Oz* in their household.

There wasn't a second of violence in the original *Beauty and the Beast* that disturbed her. For some reason, the Beast—whom I would have found pretty formidable when I was her age, doesn't haunt her. And Belle. Her major goal in life is to *be* Belle. Thanks to twelve doting aunts and uncles, Belle is branded on Tori's underwear, nightgown, slippers, toothbrush, lamp, sheets, sleeping bag, and costumes, not to mention her plain old toys.

The one thing she doesn't have and is salivating to own is the upcoming sequel. Sequels to all of these fairy tales make liars out of the endings of the books and videos: "And they lived happily ever after. . . . THE END." With the Disney Company's appreciation for the unlimited marketing possibilities of extending stories into sequels, there's now no such thing as a simple "happily ever after."

For weeks, Tori has been tracking the weekly progress of the newest *Beauty and the Beast*—masterfully timed for release right before Christmas. With three weeks to go, Tori and I have long-standing plans to make a gingerbread house, shop for her family Christmas presents, wrap them, eat a pizza, and then, the *pièce de résistance*, watch the *Beauty and the Beast* sequel I'd bought earlier in the week. I am still embarrassed that I stood in line, freezing my ass off with a number of mothers until ten when the Video Warehouse opens. I didn't do things like this for Keara. I am going to be an incredibly indulgent grandmother.

Tori is as excited as I've ever seen. The video starts off great. The singing and dancing kitchen utensils never looked better. Belle looks like a million bucks. But then a creepy addition threatens to ruin the mood. A rather imposing pipe organ plays scary music like a player piano. Watching it, I'm hoping the organ is just establishing some ominous presence, not any kind of culprit on its own. Tori slowly begins to slide beneath the afghan we're cuddled under. Within thirty seconds she is totally submerged.

"Turn it off," I hear her little voice plead. "Turn the organ off," she repeats.

"Honey it's only a musical instrument"—albeit an increasingly large and leering pipe organ—"It can't hurt anybody."

"Please . . . turn it off *NOW*!"

I turn it off.

"Now, rewind it," she commands. She's still totally under the blanket.

"Okay."

"Now put it in the box," she directs me as if I'm handling poison.

"Yeah."

"Okay, put it in the bag it came in."

"All done. Now what would you like watch?" I ask.

"It's in the box? And the bag?"

"Yeah."

"Bring it downstairs."

"Downstairs?"

"Yeah. Now."

"Tori, it doesn't make any difference. It's not showing."

"PLEEAASSEE."

"Okay." I run down and throw it on the dining room table. I run back upstairs. She's still under the blanket.

"Hey, I've got an idea. Let's watch *The Sound of Music*."

"Okay," she relents.

Maria hasn't even fully expressed her wonder that the "hills are alive," when Tori, who is clinging to me, whispers, "Take it outside."

"What?"

"The tape."

"Outside? Where?"

"Throw it away."

"Tori, I'm not going to throw away a brand-new video. Who knows, you might like it in a week. How about I put it in the trunk of one of the cars? I'll cover it with a bunch of junk and then lock it all up."

"Okay," she says meekly.

I run out front and bury the tape in my trunk. I glance up and there is her concerned little face poking through the curtains, making sure I keep my promise.

"I need to call my mom."

"Okay."

She whispers into the phone, then says, "My mom wants to talk to you."

"Marth, I'm going to come get her," Rachel says.

"Rachel, that's an hour each way. Don't you think I can get her calmed down?"

"No."

"The organ was a little creepy but . . . You don't think she'll stay? Listen, you've got to get Gracie to bed. Brian and I will bring her back."

"Thanks."

"Tori, we're going home," I tell her.

"What car?"

"Brian's car."

"Not *your* car?"

"No, not my car."

"That's where the video is."

"I know. Don't worry. It's going to stay there."

Once we get on the road and the distance grows between her and the offending video, she becomes more engaged in talking about Christmas. But when we get to her house, she hugs her parents like she's a released hostage.

We visit for a while.

Tori comes down in her pj's to say good night, which interestingly are *Little Mermaid* ones. No *Beauty and the Beast* in evidence. I hug her and tell her everyone has stuff that scares them and the next time she sleeps over, we'll make sure we only watch things we've seen before. I notice her flinch when I say, *"Next time you sleep over."* Her nod seems closer to saying *when hell freezes over* than any true assent that she will ever set foot in my house again.

THE CALL

*A*fter several days of slow progress on my badly neglected to-do list, the notation, *Call re: Santa program* has risen to first place and can no longer be ignored. I reluctantly dial the number on the rumpled shelter newsletter, ready with an obsessive list of questions, drawing a deep breath in preparation for talking to someone I don't know. Instead, I get a recording of a clipped, efficient voice thanking me for my interest in the program. She instructs me to leave my name and number with the promise that I will be contacted by a staff member as soon as possible. I could hang up right now and technically cross another entry off the list. But, hell, it's Christmas.

"Yeah, hi," I say at the beep. "This is Martha Manning. I got one of your flyers and I wanted to see what was involved" (translation: how much work and money?) "in the Adopt-a-Family Christmas program. Can you give me a call when you get a chance?" I leave my name and number and hang up.

These people waste no time. Less than an hour later there

is an enthusiastic message from a woman who sounds like we're best friends.

"Hi, Martha. We're so happy that you volunteered for our program," she chirps. *(I did?)* "Welcome! In a day or two you will get the wish list of one of our families. Then all you have to do is get the gifts, wrap them, and drop them here at the shelter. We'll deliver them to the family. Call if you have any questions. Bye-bye!" In the span of sixty seconds I've become Santa to a bunch of people I don't know in a program I know next to nothing about.

The letter arrives in the mail so promptly the next day that I check for a postmark to see whether it had been dropped off rather than mailed to avoid my backing out. The list was filled out in pencil by a woman named Tracy Raina Grant— mother of a two-year-old daughter and two-month-old twin sons. Straightforward, precise, and very practical, the biggest-ticket item is a sturdy Fisher-Price table and chair set for children. Everything was for the kids with the exception of a pair of boots from Lady Foot Locker. Unlike the things for the kids about which their mother Tracy Raina was so exact, the information about the boots is vague, the style and size written so lightly I can't decipher them. It was almost as if she were less sure about asking for herself. I do everything I can think of— hold it up to the light at various angles, get Brian's opinion. Nothing. I break down and do what I should have done in the beginning—call the shelter for clarification.

"Arlington Homeless Shelter." A hassled voice on the other end.

"Hi. This is Martha Manning."

"Uh-huh." She's definitely not one of the friendly recruitment staff.

"I'm doing the Santa Adopt-a-Family program."

"That's great," she says like she's trying to be enthusiastic, but it feels like she wants to blurt out *What do you want, the Volunteer of the Year award?* "Is there a problem?" she asks condescendingly.

"I wouldn't really call it a problem exactly. Except y'know those wish lists? I can't read the writing about a pair of boots the mom wants."

"And how is that a problem?"

"Well, I want to give her the right size and style, the ones she asked for."

The seconds of silence tell me she is not appreciating my dilemma and also give me the opportunity to kick myself for ever getting involved in what I expected would be the closest available thing to drive-by charity.

"I'm still not clear what you need from me."

"Oh!" I'm so relieved we're back on track. "I was thinking that you could just ask her what she wrote so we could get it cleared up."

"Tracy Raina Grant and her family moved today to transitional housing in an apartment complex. Her phone should be in tomorrow. You can give her a call. . . . Just wait one sec . . . I'll find her number."

"Hold on, hold on," I interject. "I was hoping someone from your place would call her. See, I don't even know her—"

Triumphant, she interrupts me. "Here you go! I knew I had it somewhere." She gives me the phone number. "Okay? Good. Bye-bye."

"But—" I'm getting close to begging.

Click.

I get one more idea that may help me avoid actually meeting the family I have "adopted." Lady Foot Locker isn't too far from our house. I drive to the local mall and ask a saleswoman dressed like a referee to arbitrate my confusion with the list. We narrow it down to two styles of boot, but they're very different. Her vision is no sharper than mine when it comes to deciphering the size. She encourages me to just take a guess, but Tracy Raina asked for only that one thing. It has to be right.

There's no choice. I've got to call her. When it comes to talking to people I don't know, I am full of contradictions — great in front of one thousand and terrible at a party in a circle of four. Over the past years I've become more private, most comfortable in my own house, secure in the familiar boundaries of family and friends. My idea of a perfect charity is being able to help people without having anything to do with them. It sounds flippant, but it's painfully true. In every volunteer situation in which I've been the helper coming face-to-face with the helpee, it has always been awkward. It doesn't matter whether it's dishing out food at soup kitchens, passing out groceries on street corners, or listening to women describe in a language that is foreign to me — but in a tone of pain that is all too familiar — their lives in refugee camps. I become inundated by shame for my relatively privileged position on the yardstick of need, then paralyzed by the paltry efforts I am making to change the position of a single person on the other end of that ruler.

Arlington Homeless Shelter has broken the contract of built-in distance for this do-gooder. I have no choice, I tell myself, as I clench my teeth and dial Raina's number.

Four rings . . . that's enough . . . hang up, I'm telling myself as someone picks up the phone.

"Hello. This is Martha Manning. May I please speak with Tracy Raina?"

"This is her."

Oh God. She sounds black. Why wouldn't she be? But Tracy Raina sounds like such a white-girl name, which I realize makes absolutely no sense at all.

In that moment our greetings are secondary to sizing each other up. Not only can I tell she is black. I'm certain she can tell I'm not. I feel like lily white Lady Bountiful, which at one point in history might have felt pretty good, but at this point in time feels like crap. For a moment I consider identifying myself as the gas meter lady, calling to arrange a reading, but then I reconsider.

"Hi. I'm doing the Santa Adopt-a-Family program and I got your family" *(Oh God . . . I am so awkward)* "and everything's fine, but I'm having trouble with the boots." The breath is not fully out of my mouth before she cuts me off.

"Oh, you don't have to get them."

"No, no," I cut in. "It's just that I couldn't make out your handwriting on the list so I couldn't tell which kind of boots you wanted—or the size. I had it down to between two kinds."

"The ones I was thinking of," she offers tentatively, "are mostly tan with dark-brown trim."

"I know *exactly* the ones you mean." I'm all excited that we click.

"Did you go over there?" she asks.

"Yeah, I wanted to be sure to get the right ones. They look really comfortable."

Sounds of babies fussing, kids playing, and adults talking, combined with the moving of boxes and furniture make it hard to hear.

"Oh! Tracy Raina, I almost forgot. I need your shoe size."

"They gave you the name Tracy Raina?" She laughs.

"Yeah. Is that wrong?"

"It's just Raina. Tracy is my first name, but I don't use it."

"Okay."

"Now my shoe size, that's a problem." She chuckles. "Since I had my twins my shoe size isn't back to normal and who knows if it will ever get there."

"When I had my daughter, I gained a whole shoe size and I kept waiting for it to go back."

"How old is your daughter?"

"Nineteen," I say before I realize I have just put myself solidly in the middle-aged category.

"How long did it take to get your shoe size back?" she asks.

"Well, I'm still optimistic. . . ."

She has a great laugh. It sings. There's something so freeing about sharing a laugh with someone. It opens invisible doors between strangers.

"I just had my gallbladder removed, so there's swelling from that," she says as she tries to calculate her new size. "Let's say eight and a half. I can always exchange them."

"Wait a minute," I break in. "You have two-month-old twins, a two-year-old, just had a gallbladder operation, and you just moved?"

"Yeah." She sighs.

"Wow! Did you see the gallbladder coming?"

"No, but bad gallbladders run in my family. So do twins."

"Jeez . . . within a couple of weeks of each other . . . plus the move . . ."

"You know what they say," she reminds me. "God never gives you more than you can handle."

The 24/7 cynical ticker tape that runs in my head spells out *And you believe . . .*

"Yeah, but your family does," I quip. "I read that somewhere," I add, to lessen the sacrilege.

Fortunately she is chuckling, almost in spite of herself.

We've come to the end of the road in our conversation.

She was polite.

I was polite.

It was awful.

"So, anyway," I conclude, "if you think of anything else just leave me a message. Here's my number."

Since the shelter will be delivering the gifts I assume this will be our first and last conversation, I wish her Merry Christmas, to which she replies "God's blessing on you."

I have no idea how to respond, so I say something lame like "Yeah, you, too." We say our tentative, uncomfortable good-byes.

I get some Christmas shopping momentum going and start having fun. Having not really shopped for girls' clothes for six years, it is a blast to play with kids' clothes and toys—even the baby boy stuff. I've missed Christmas shopping for Keara. She still gets lots of gifts, but the word "shopping" no longer applies. Now I fulfill a detailed inventory with absolutely nothing left to chance. Now we have very different tastes. Keara is less likely to dismiss our differences as merely a gap between two people's tastes. It's Keara's assessment that she is all taste and I have absolutely none. So I supplement her totally boring Christmas list with some surprises usually related to childrens' literature—a love we thankfully still share.

Raina's two-year-old daughter, Jade's, girly-girl wishes still leave room for my imagination. Shopping for the twins is delightful and takes me way, way back.

I have to go to four different stores before finding the Fisher-Price table set. They are apparently very popular, because the stores want to give out rain checks. They make it sound so easy. All you have to do is convince millions of children to believe that putting off something they *really* want till after Christmas in exchange for a 10 percent discount is a great idea. The first problem is that most kids have no appreciation of the whole percentage-discount concept. Much more serious is the dent it puts in the whole Santa Claus belief system.

Not only do I have the gifts but they're wrapped with thirty-six hours to spare. I'm usually trying to get a present wrapped while driving to the place of gift giving. I'm much more at ease with my next call to the shelter.

"Hello, Arlington Shelter." I know that voice. It's the hassled, unhelpful lady. "Hi, this is Martha Manning," I say with considerably more confidence than during my last call. "I'm participating in the Christmas program—"

"Giving or getting?" she butts in. *God, this woman has no patience.*

"Giving," I say, a little put out that she couldn't somehow tell automatically.

"Yes?" she says in her get-to-the-point tone.

"I put together the gifts, and I wanted to know what the hours are for dropping them off and where I should bring them."

"Your name?" she demands.

"Manning."

"Manning . . . Okay, you have the Grant family."

"Yes. I know that. I just want to drop the gifts off at the shelter. What would be a good time . . . ? Oh, and I need directions."

"Well, they've moved into transitional housing—an apartment. They're not here anymore."

"That's okay," I reassure her. "I'll just drop the stuff off and you can get it to her." No answer—I hear her shuffling papers. Suddenly she perks up. "Ms. Manning? Good news! I'm looking at a map and you actually live much closer to Ms. Grant than to us . . . about a mile and a half . . . practically on the same street."

"Yeah?" I'm not sure what difference that makes. "I just need to know when to drop this off at the *shelter*, like it said in the flyer."

All of a sudden, she's really nice. "Ms. Manning, we are *so* backed up here. It would be so helpful if you could just give Ms. Grant a call and arrange to deliver the gifts yourself."

There is *no* way to win here. I can start insisting that I did my part of the program and they haven't come through with theirs, but that would sound whiny and entitled. *Damn her.*

"Okay, give me her number again," I say, resigned.

She repeats it several times, then provides the address. She was right about how close we live. It couldn't be a straighter shot—just down my street and a right turn to her apartment complex.

"Merry Christmas, Ms. Manning," she says brightly.

"Yeah, you, too," I respond with considerably less enthusiasm.

I dial Raina's number.

Three rings.

"Hello."

"Hi, this is Martha. Can I talk to Raina?"

"Hold on." Not exactly welcoming—like I'm a bill collector or a social worker or some other white woman who wants something.

"Raina!" the woman yells.

I try to get her attention. I hear her put the phone down.

Another woman comes to the phone. "Hello," a different voice, somewhat cold.

"Raina?"

"Yeah."

"This is Martha Manning. I talked—"

"Oh yeah. Hi."

"I just talked to the woman at the shelter, and she said that instead of their staff bringing the gifts that I should bring the Christmas stuff over to your place myself. I wasn't sure what a good time would be."

"Oh, things are pretty disorganized," she says apologetically. "We just moved in. . . ."

"I won't stay. They just said you and I live closer to each other than the shelter."

"Where are you?"

"On South George Mason. Y'know Alcova Park?"

"Oh yeah."

"I live right across from there."

"Okay, so you know how to get here. You need to get buzzed in." She gives me the code I will need to punch in. The noise, blending baby sounds and music playing, is escalating.

"Could you be quiet?" she calls out.

"How are you?" I ask.

"Well, the healing is better. I'm real, real tired. The babies are so cute. I put their little seats facing toward each other and it's like they try to talk to each other. It is so funny. You'll see them when you come."

"What would be the best time for you?"

"I'll be here all day. Come anytime," she says calmly, despite two wailing infants in the background. "Come anytime" she repeats in the first of what will become hundreds of invitations. "I'll be here."

"Okay, how about two-thirty?"

"Good. I'll put the babies down."

We Meet

*B*efore I ask Brian to help carry the Adopt-a-Family gifts to the station wagon, I make one surreptitious, very loaded trip of my own. I'm trying to spare him the knowledge of the exact cost of my volunteerism. Never mind that I am really trying to spare myself. Either way, this accounting confrontation is better put off until January.

The secret trip to the car turns out to have been a good idea, because on his second trip down the steps he yells out, "My God, how many families did you adopt?" I pretend he's too far away and I don't hear him.

When I get down to the car, I say innocently, "Honey, doesn't it feel great, in a culture of such selfishness, to be doing something so good for someone else?"

In these moments I recall years of report cards—the ones that said *Martha has excellent verbal skills*. I always wonder if that included the *use* of those skills in such manipulative ways. Brian immediately realizes that he's been cornered by a question he can't answer. He lamely nods, and then I throw in Part Two. "Y'know, honey, if it *is* too much, please take it out of my Christmas this year. *I mean it*. There's nothing I really want that I don't already have." This falls into the Big Fat Lie category. If I come down on Christmas morning and find a lonely card that says *Your Christmas gift this year is everything you gave away— exactly as you asked*, I will be royally pissed. I *want* to be a generous person. I have moments of true humility, pure heartbeats of perfect selflessness. But they never last. I always end up comparing myself to people I deem less kind. I puff up at the prospect of my own goodness. I find myself counting up whatever membership reward points I need for whatever program gets me closer to the ultimate in travel—Heaven. By then, I've ruined my good intentions.

Once everything is packed in the car, I invite Brian along, "to help me unload." He draws the line.

"Martha," he sighs with thirty years of experience, "you don't *need* help, you just don't want to go *alone*." I consider protesting, but he's got me nailed.

"Okay, you're right, I don't. *But please come.*"

"Nope." He drops the keys in my hand. "You didn't ask me when you volunteered, but now all of a sudden you want me with you. Go on. You'll be fine."

His selfishness turns out to be unexpectedly helpful. On the drive to Raina's, I am so busy muttering and mumbling about what a heathen Brian is—despite the fact he attends weekly Mass and sings in the choir—and what a saint I am—despite the fact that I don't do either—there's no time to be consumed by anxiety. It is a welcome escape from my routine panic in new situations, meeting new people—lacking a playbook to tell me how to act. I take a right into a complex of low-rise brick garden apartments. They called them "garden" twenty-five years ago when *we* were first married, and "gardens" are in no more evidence now than they were then. Finding Raina's building is no problem. Getting *into* it is an entirely different story. There's a three-digit apartment code Raina said to look up on the console outside her building that will give me the two-digit number to dial to get buzzed in. But once I'm standing at the door, the proper order of those numbers totally eludes me. I knock on the outside door awhile. No luck. So I start pushing buttons, only to end up pissing off several people I mistakenly buzz repeatedly.

Finally, I spot a young couple all dressed up, carrying holiday shopping bags down the stairs and toward the front door.

They give me the once-over, decide that I mean no harm, and hold the door open for me. I'm brimming with gifts and so damn glad to be *in*, I begin to thank them by launching into an explanation of my dilemma, a confession of lousy memory, and much more. The young man nods politely for a few seconds but then gently cuts me off with *"Feliz Navidad."* The young woman repeats it. It's clear they neither understand nor care about my troubles. Hell, what I just babbled probably made no sense in *English*.

"Gracias." I smile back. It was all that ever needed saying.

The next hurdle. I climb the steps to Raina's door, behind which I can hear a lot going on. A contentious TV talk show is on loud. It sounds like there are more than three kids and they are all making their presence known. *Oh God. I wish I could just drop the gifts, press the doorbell, and dash away, like some prankster on Halloween.* Then I try a good mental kick in the ass that sometimes works: *Oh grow up!*

I knock. No answer. Again. Louder. A woman answers the door, not too happily.

"Raina?" I ask.

"Who do you want?" she asks. *Oh God, I'm at the wrong apartment!*

"Raina Grant?"

"Raina!" she yells, then plops down to watch TV on a long couch where two babies in matching infant seats sit facing each other. Not identical, they are equally adorable. This young woman leaves me standing there in the midst of unpacked boxes, stacks of clothes, diapers, sheets, and blankets.

"Hi. I'm Martha," I address her optimistically.

"Hi," she responds flatly, denying me her name.

I am embarrassed. I wonder if she is, too.

Another woman enters the room, negotiating the minefield

of a newly moved-into apartment. Raina is attractive, in her late twenties or early thirties, fighting the same pounds in some of the same places I am. Her long hair is pulled straight back into a ponytail. She is pale beneath her light brown skin. Under her eyes are the puffy I'd-kill-for-sleep dark circles of new mothers. With the exception of her fuzzy house slippers, we are dressed alike in gray sweat suits.

As she fumbles around to make room for me to sit, she introduces me to sons Darren and Deven, both in green terry cloth jumpsuits, hair already long, huge brown eyes, matching runny noses, and pacifiers that are getting an Olympic workout. Raina introduces me to her cousin Kayla, who stopped by to see the kids. She says hi again, but doesn't lift her eyes from the TV. Raina notices me looking around and is right on the money about what I'm thinking. "Oh, my daughter, Jade, is out with the children's father." This raises more questions for me than answers. *He's not her husband, not her boyfriend, not her . . . anything.* I'm thinking, *But with a two-year-old and two-month-old twins he has to have been something to her.*

She's frowning from sharing just that little information about him, so my guess is that there's been recent heartbreak.

Babies are a great conversational lubricant. I am grateful for the twins, who are not just politely cute but absolutely engaging. I play peekaboo with them and shake their rattles while carrying on a conversation with Raina full of "sisterhood" questions — labor, pain, birth, stitches, breast feeding, and sleeping through the night. She finishes with the challenge of their frequent respiratory infections. I am an open door when it comes to any germ that can settle in and make life miserable. I do a quick inventory of the close encounters I've just had with their little noses and fingers and wheezy little lungs. I'll be sick within two days.

After Raina and I have unloaded the station wagon, she is

overwhelmed by the haul. As she rearranges the bags of gifts, I spot a Fisher-Price table and chair set fully assembled and already in use—covered with the remains of a macaroni-and-cheese lunch and a box of apple juice.

"There's an envelope at the bottom of one of the bags with all the receipts," I try to say tactfully.

She interrupts with reassurance. "Oh, I won't need them. I'm sure everything is fine."

I wince and point to the large wrapped square with the big box next to it.

Recognizing its contents, she puts her hand over her mouth and laughs.

"Unless you're planning to have quadruplets in the next few months," I joke, "you might want to make an exchange."

"Oh no! I can't believe it! Y'know I was just talking to my girlfriend and she said the Fisher-Price stuff was selling out fast. I had this gift certificate, so I ran over and got the *very last one* at Target."

"So that was *you*?" I tease.

She laughs again, gently slapping my shoulder.

For the first time in this visit I feel like myself. Not my white middle-class Santa stand-in self. Just my *plain old self*.

"There's so much I can exchange it for. Did you see all the accessories?"

"Yeah." I nod. "It all looks so sturdy . . . and practical." This marks the official end of our conversation. I've run out of things to say. Raina is about as much of a small talker as I am.

And Kayla certainly isn't rushing to help us through. I look at my watch like I'm a very busy woman on a tight schedule. "I'd better get going," I say.

"Thank you so much," she says as she opens the door. There's a surge of energy—enough for a hug. But we pull back and settle for an awkward handshake.

I climb back into my car feeling self-conscious and uncomfortable. I feel so white. In these situations, I never know if I'm paranoid or right or both. I don't have a single close black friend. I have acquaintances, work companions, but not the kind of relationship you can get low down with—someone who'll tell you if your ass looks fat in the dress or that what you just said is the dumbest thing she's ever heard. I try to shake off the discomfort of the visit with the knowledge that I did a good thing and the reassurance that I never have to do it again.

COLOR BLINDNESS

I can't help thinking about Raina and Kayla, the unfriendly cousin. Did I bring the discomfort along with me, or was it there already, waiting to be activated, like some detonation device, when the right—or in this case, wrong—components came together? For me, it's the feeling of being white. I'm always white, but I don't feel it unless it contributes to a sense of "otherness," a sense that I don't belong. For a long time mine was an innocent arrogance: I was somehow color-blind; race didn't matter.

The first good kick I got in that assumption happened immediately after the O. J. Simpson verdict was announced. Two minutes afterward, the black FedEx guy who'd been working in my neighborhood for the past couple of years, knocked on our door. Having been glued to the TV I wasn't sure I wanted to get it. But a quick glance out the window and I knew I needed to sign for a delivery. Plus, I had a pleasant relationship with him. Not sure they were allowed radios in their trucks, I couldn't wait to tell him the outcome of the trial.

I opened the door. Before he could hand me my envelope

or the clipboard for signing, I asked breathlessly, "Did you hear the verdict?"

"Yeah," he said, shaking his head. "Unbelievable."

"I know."

I started to sign my name on the clipboard. "I mean, the guy is guilty as *sin*."

He gave me a look—a double take. "You're kidding, right?"

All of a sudden, he's an attractive black man in his twenties and I'm a slobby white woman almost twice his age.

"You don't think he killed those people?" I pressed him.

He put his hand up to stop me as he punched in his information on the portable computer he carried. "That's not the point," he said between beeps.

"Well, then what is?"

He took the clipboard, checked my signature, and looked me in the eye with a look that said *No hard feelings*.

Over the next few weeks it became clear that the FedEx guy was not alone in his feelings about the O. J. trial. The verdict touched a deep fault line that exists in this country about race—an issue that transcends education, income, and class.

But it wasn't our discussion in those brief moments that has stayed with me for so long. As he began his walk toward his truck, he turned around. "That could never happen to me."

I look at him as if to say *What are you talking about?*

He held out the computerized tracking device in his hands. "This thing accounts for me every second of the day. No one"—and he waved the device up and down my street—"could ever get away with accusing me of doing something I didn't do. I always have proof of where I am." I didn't immediately understand his meaning.

"This conversation isn't over," I called as he crossed the street to his truck.

He held up his hand in affirmation.

Our interaction was like sand in my bathing suit for the entire day. It was like the punch line to a joke everyone found funny and I still didn't get. I kept thinking about that computer he carried and how pleased he was to have it. Then it began to dawn. And then it hit. The machine was there to track packages, *not people*. Yet to him, it was his omnipresent witness, a ready alibi should someone in an unfriendly neighborhood unjustly accuse him. I became aware of a disturbing fact: that when it comes to race *I don't even know what I* don't *know*.

Confirmation of that fact was compounded a year later when I appeared on a panel about memoirs with a professor from Morehouse College. The other people on the panel were either flaky or puffed-up, dull academics. The final contributor, a woman regal in African headdress and robes, not only wrote beautifully but her delivery was also breathtaking. I didn't know anyone at the conference, and there was a cocktail party for authors that night. I waited for her to finish with the well-wishers and autograph seekers. I don't appear shy, but I really am. Once I got my turn, I was nervous.

"Hi, Dr. Rice. I'm Martha Manning. I was on the panel with you. I've loved your work."

She laughed. "I know. You're funny," she answered, referring to my reading.

"Thanks. Listen, are you going to the authors' reception tonight?"

She frowned. "I hate those things."

"Me, too," I agreed. "I don't know about you, but I'm here on my publisher's dime . . . and we do have to eat dinner. . . ."

She brightened up. "Have you seen the revolving restaurant on the top of the hotel?"

"I bet it's *reeaally* expensive." I laughed.

She shared the pleasure of putting the screws to a publisher —

any publisher. "We better call right away for reservations," she said as she walked toward a house phone on the wall. In a moment, "mission accomplished." She apologized for all that was left—5:30. Old-lady hours, I called them, but pronounced them perfect, silently figuring that it was early enough that one or both of us could pretend we were going to the reception or somewhere else if dinner was awful. And if we hit it off, well, the reservation says when to come, but *nothing* about when we have to *go*.

We sat in that restaurant for four hours. The conversation flowed in and out of one subject to another—religion, publishers, writing, motherhood, working at a traditionally black versus Ivy League college versus state school. We could talk forever.

We began to talk about our kids and she happened to mention that her son lives in Arlington, Virginia, where I live. He's a young attorney, working in the city, and he usually commuted to work by subway. A voracious reader, he traveled back and forth with a backpack full of work and library books. I couldn't put my finger on it immediately, but I suddenly noticed my charming dinner companion has stiffened. Her voice sounded harder, strained. *"Arlington, Virginia,"* she repeated.

"Yeah." I chattered on. "I love living so close to the city. It's a pretty place, and it's so diverse. You can get any kind of food without leaving the town."

"Diverse?" she asked sharply.

"Well, in South Arlington, where I live, it is. Then there's the more upscale North Arlington." There were several beats of silence like she was evaluating whether to pursue this conversation.

She put down her wineglass, and leaned forward. Her voice was strong but slightly shaking. "One night, in *Arlington, Virginia*," she began, "my son was coming home from work. He had changed into his running clothes before he left work, his backpack was full of books, and when he got off at his Metro stop, he slapped on his headphones and started his usual jog toward home through the residential area he always ran in. Out of nowhere, these police cars pulled up. The cops yelled at him to stop, and he had no idea they were even addressing him, so he just kept going. They grabbed him, wrestled him to the ground, his head on the cement held by one cop, his hands restrained with cuffs by another." Dr. Rice's mellow voice turned steely as she continued. "When my son asked what was going on, they told him to shut up. He couldn't reach for his wallet to give his ID. Any protests were met with more hostility from the officers."

"My God. It sounds like a Kafka story."

"You got that, sister," she agreed. "They kept calling for backup. *For what? For protection against my son?* I wish you could see him. You'd know what I mean." She reached into her bag, flipped open her wallet, and pointed to a beaming face in cap and gown, the photo taken at his law school graduation. I can see what she means. Maybe it's just the mother in me, but I saw a sweetness in him. There was nothing to say. I just nodded.

"Anyway, my son kept asking what he was accused of. He told them he's an attorney several times, and actually had the nerve several times to bring up rights-related issues. They were unimpressed, like he was lying. Finally they admitted that someone 'fitting his description' with a backpack had committed armed robbery. They were dumping the contents of his backpack all over the trunk of a squad car, making jokes about his having so many books, that he probably knocked over some libraries. Somehow, despite the fact that he told them he's an attorney, they try to find some deeper meaning in the folded suit in the bag, as if it is proof of something sinister.

"Several long minutes later, a call came through on the radio from the dispatcher, confirming that they'd found the robber. An officer uncuffed him, stood him up, and said, 'You're okay. You can get going. Sometimes these things happen.' The nicer of the cops told him that a series of victims had described the robber as a 'black man running with a backpack'—which was apparently all that was involved in the criteria of 'fitting his description.' They drove off without even an apology. He stood there shaking and started to sob."

As his mother told the story, it was clear she was reliving it herself. "When he called me sobbing—my beautiful, sweet boy . . ." She trailed off. The thought of my daughter who walks or runs from the New York subway at all hours of the day and night being stopped like that, pushed down, head held to the ground and not knowing *why, why, why* made me feel sick to my stomach. I was ashamed of where I lived, this supposedly enlightened place. And I was puzzled. Did these things happen all the time? I'd always believed reports I'd read about racial profiling and DWBs (driving while black) but I relegated their occurrence to big cities and long stretches of lonely Southern roads.

I was well aware of that particular, quiet neighborhood, the winding street of brick colonials, understated landscaping with the appropriate flowers for every season, Volvos and minivans in the driveways. Mothers and fathers walked to the Metro from these houses. How does he recover whatever innocence he has left by his late twenties when it is annihilated in less than five minutes in an absolutely lovely neighborhood?

THANK YOU

$\mathcal{T}$hree weeks after Christmas, the phone rings. I don't recognize the number on the caller ID—my protection against
distraction while I'm writing—so I let the answering machine
pick up. A woman, with a voice that is vaguely familiar, begins
to leave a message.

"Oh hi. This is Raina. From Christmas. I've been meaning
to call you before this, but, well, things have been crazy."

I sit there listening, a debate raging in my head. *Pick up, talk
to her versus just let her say thank you and clear the decks.*

"Anyway . . . ," she continues.

I pick up.

"Raina?"

"Yeah. Hi." She stutters. It sounds like she was glad she
was talking to an answering machine and I've just thrown her
off course.

"Hi," I say. "How are you?"

"Oh, you know. Really busy."

"I can imagine."

"I was calling to thank you for everything from Christmas.
I tried to get your address because I wrote you a thank-you
note, but the shelter hasn't called me back. I tried to get your
address out of the phone book, but I couldn't find your name."

"Oh, we're listed under my husband's last name—
Depenbrock."

"You have a different last name?"

"Yeah, I kept my maiden name."

"Oh."

"How was your Christmas?" I ask.

"It was really nice. The twins didn't know what was going

on, but Jade loved it all. I love the boots and the bath oil and everything else."

"I'm so glad . . . oh, did you exchange the Fisher-Price table and chair set?"

"Oh yeah, and with the after-Christmas sales I got good deals on winter clothes for the boys and some learning toys for Jade. She already knows some of her ABCs."

We are like two people just learning how to play tennis. Each exchange, each volley, takes so much fumbling and effort to complete. There's a your-turn, my-turn quality to our conversation that makes it seem forced, and yet there's a corresponding wish to keep going, to endure the discomfort.

"How was your Christmas?" she asks.

"Oh, it was really nice."

"Did your daughter—what is her name—come home?"

"Keara. Yeah, she was home for ten days. It was so good to have her home. When she leaves, it makes me realize how much I've missed her since she's been in college. My parents live in Rockville and I have five brothers and sisters. With their kids, it's pretty much a zoo, but I love it," I tell her.

Raina chuckles. "Oh, you have a big family, too. I've got two sisters and two brothers. We did the same thing."

Silence.

"Raina, I was thinking about you and wondering how you were, but I felt like if I called you might think I was being nosy."

"What?" She laughs. "That's not true."

"I really wanted to meet Jade, and Brian wanted to meet you. But I didn't want to butt in."

"That's silly."

"Well, what I wanted to tell you was that if you ever need a baby-sitter, I'd love to do it. I'm really missing kids. I work at home and my schedule is pretty flexible so, well, just keep me in mind."

"Okay. Thanks."

"I'm really glad you called."

"Me, too. Thank you again. For everything."

"Believe me, it was a pleasure."

"Bye."

"Bye."

HESITATION

$\mathcal{F}$ollowing Raina's thank-you call to me, I wait two weeks before calling her back. Our conversation begins stilted and awkward, but in trading the details of our lives—mostly the day-to-day stuff—we usually end up sharing some laughs, the strongest cement to set a fledgling friendship. Missing Keara who's at college, I repeat that I am happy to baby-sit if she wants to get out by herself. She always politely replies that she appreciates it. But she has her mother, two sisters, and a niece who live within a couple of miles.

At my most suspicious I think she wants evidence of my mothering ability and I can't wait for her to meet Keara.

Raina and I tiptoe around each other for several months. It feels like those torturous junior high school dances—where the boys cluster on one side, the girls on the other. The music plays, the invitation to break free from the safety of the pack to venture into the wide, empty middle space, make a claim on someone of the opposite sex—it's all so appealing. The yearning for connection is palpable. But so is the awkward anxiety. That yearning, despite the possibility of rejection and embarrassment, is a magnetic power that keeps everyone glued to floor, safe in their wanting.

The music keeps playing for Raina and me. And every now and then we venture forth for a quick dance. But we quickly retreat into our corners wondering if we are at the end of something small or the beginning of something big.

WALKING THE TIGHTROPE

*W*hen it comes to paying for the roofs over our heads, many of us walk a tightrope monthly. For some, it is a relentless and frightening walk—counting nickels and dimes, knowing that the voices of "Mr. Smith" or "Mrs. Walker" on their answering machines are far less friendly than their generically common names would suggest. Then there's the scanning for the unfamiliar numbers momentarily inscribed on caller ID, calls that should not be answered. Every month it is the same—we must maintain our balance to make that walk toward security and stability.

Most of the time you reach the end of the month safe in your house with whatever source of cash that's still keeping you afloat—even if you've just barely managed to get by. You haven't lost your balance and spilled your guts on the pavement, but you haven't moved a centimeter closer to your material dreams and goals either. The relief each month is intense but momentary—you soon realize that the rope suspended over the pit of debt, insecurity, plunging credit, homelessness, and poverty down below, waits for you to make the inevitable walk back in thirty days.

That's what surviving is—just making the walk back and

forth without falling. And it happens at all income levels but with different results.

Sometimes you launch into the monthly tightrope walk purposely—in the service of some great but expensive goal—college, graduate school, a home, some aspiration in which all but one dream is deferred. There is some beautiful picture of what lies at the other end that will make this craziness worth it. It's like you collect a chip for each walk across the tightrope and all the chips add up over the years it takes you to become, get, or own something. Sometimes you search your pockets, the change dish on your desk, and under the couch cushions for the three bucks to cover a regular burger and a small cola, and you can't get it together. You can't pull off something that wasn't worth a second thought when you were ten. You find yourself frequently telling yourself and each other that someday you'll look back on these times and laugh. Yeah, right. I'm still waiting.

But there's another, much more important difference between all of us tightrope walkers. *Our nets.*

As I get to know Raina, I nod in limited recognition at her scraping together the quarters she needs so she can do the laundry in the apartment house basement. I can see myself in her anxiety about whether she is going to have the cash together on the day the rent is due. As much as I can feel the strain of the mental gymnastics that come from wondering what check will clear by when, factoring in the grace periods before they threaten to turn off the gas, water, phone, electricity and when they actually do it. Or praying that your kid's sniffles won't get worse, not just because of your maternal sympathies but because of the major domino effect that even a minor ear infection can set off—when everyone in the family gets sick and the kids aren't able to go to child care, even though you still have to pay for it. You can't go to work and your sick leave has long been used up, rarely due to your own illness. And then, of course, there are the doctor's fees and the cost of medicine. It's one of those aspects of parenthood that never gets easier with more experience. Then there's that damn molar on the right side—the one that by late afternoon is going to be making you want to grab a pair of pliers and launch into personal dentistry. Not to mention that the clunking in your car engine is probably more than an interesting alternative to your car radio.

Then there are the nighttime worries—the ticker tape, like on the stock exchange or the news, that constantly runs along the bottom of your thoughts—that keeps you up at night. There's the Brownie uniform your daughter is going to need next month. The gift she's going to have to bring to the birthday party she's invited to on Saturday. And the seemingly excess growth hormones that always seem to end up in your son's feet, and he's been totally brainwashed that those feet require shoes that *must* be imprinted with the emblems endorsed by athletes who could never have afforded those shoes when *they* were kids—shoes that are the same price as small home appliances.

There are many differences between Raina and me, but one of the biggest ones is our nets. The net is different for different people. For some it is the equivalent of a trampoline—someone or something has woven a net so tightly that they will never suffer more than a short fall, with a quick and painless bounce back. I've never known that kind of rescue. My safety net is a solid middle-class family, some of whom have graduated to the upper middle class. I am blessed with a family whose ethics firmly hold that nothing is more important than the people you are related to, and you share what you have. Nothing is too small. It's not a make-it-all-better rescue ethic. The person who is falling is expected to do what's needed to get his or her life back together. But there's been enough personal struggle in my family that it's clear that sometimes it takes far longer than a month or two to get it together. And it's okay to feel bad, but not ashamed. As long as you're fighting the good fight, you deserve and will get support.

Raina has been making the tightrope walk since she was in her late teens. Her kids have a father who has not willingly offered to provide a net. Without the sense that she's going through all this for anything more than maintaining a pretty lousy status quo, she doesn't even have voices of family cheerleaders who know that "this too shall pass."

After finishing my fellowship and returning to the Washington, D.C., area with all the right letters after my name and a good, but low-paying academic job, we rented a real house in a nice-enough neighborhood near an elementary school. We were supposedly so smart but were incredibly stupid with money. We started off our professional lives with a child, already burdened with tremendous student loans times two to pay, as well as a tremendous sense of entitlement like, *Damn it, we've done everything by the numbers and we deserve to live like it. If we never have Kraft macaroni and cheese with chopped hot dogs again, it will be too soon.* And everyone was so accommodating and generous. Without even our asking, credit cards arrived in the mail every month, virginal blank checks from banks we didn't belong to. We'd go shopping for rugs or furniture, and people would tell us that we wouldn't have to spend a dime for two years. This was a wonderful world whose doors we danced and smiled our way through, seemingly without consequence.

I don't know what I would have done without that net at several painful points of my life. At two different times in our marriage, we ended up living in my parent's basement. Once, having moved back after an internship of sorts—a postcollege basic room, board, and spending money job at a drug rehab home for adolescents in rural Virginia—we were totally unprepared for having to shell out the first and last month's rent and security deposit for a very basic one-bedroom apartment in the richest county in the state. It was so much money we probably could have bought a little house with it in the area we just moved from. But we couldn't afford anything. So we lived in my parents' basement for five months, worked, and saved the money we needed for the apartment.

The longer we stayed in the renting game the harder it was to get out. Once you rent at a fixed amount for a year, you switch to month-to-month, which makes it sound like the renter and landlord are equally served. Either of you can give thirty days' notice to be out of the apartment. In the market we were renting, this arrangement served only the landlord. It was our fault for being unprepared, not having a nest egg. Actually, in our case, we had the egg before the nest. Now we had a baby and we'd already rented an apartment in Massachusetts in preparation for the high-prestige low-paying fellowship we'd be leaving for in five months.

The details aren't important. But the feeling of being at the mercy of a landlord, who sniffs out your plans to move and says "Pay up and get out" or just "Get out," is a mixture of terrified and furious. The money that you've been paying and paying for so long—doesn't make your home, your child's home, any more yours than on the day you first walked through the door and plunked the first chunk of money down.

There's no way I'm going to say I know what Raina experiences with her net, which is often made of empathy as well as very limited financial support, guaranteeing little against crashing from month to month. Living in my parents' moldy basement pseudo apartment—the place my husband and I used to sneak down to make out as teenagers—was not an aspiration of Brian's or mine.

Our net has always been there. Our parents could never pull our feet fully from the fire, just as we can't offer our grown daughter a year off, even though we would break our necks to help her out with tuition, medical care, and unexpected housing downturns.

After years it was our landlord, Earl, and his wife, Jo, who put the homeowner's bug in our ears by introducing the heart-stopping subject of staying in the house.

Oh my God, I thought, *here we go again, except now we're in even more debt and have less money to put toward house costs that have spiraled.*

Earl repeats himself. "Do you want to stay in the house?" Brian and I can't answer more quickly, and trip over each other in assent. "Yes, yes, of course, oh yeah."

"Because we were thinking that what may be holding you back is the down payment."

Bingo!

They explained the notion of renting with the option to buy, and asking if we were interested. We immediately agreed on an extra amount we would pay each month that they would hold for the down payment. It took a couple of years, but it was the first time I ever had the sense that I was actually working toward the future, a piece of the pie that wasn't ready yet but would nourish us for a long time once we had it.

The day I grew up was not the day I got married or had a baby, a Ph.D., a Harvard postdoctoral fellowship, or an academic appointment. It was when I bought a house—when I owned the wood floors, the slow drain in the upstairs bathroom, the gutters that choked from huge pine needles every season, the brick patio Earl put down himself, the gorgeous crafted molding throughout the living room. And ex-landlady Jo gave us, when we closed on the mortgage, a glass kerosene lamp from their mantel to ours—more than decorative, I thought, a wish to us for illumination and guidance, which we so badly needed.

During my most recent severe bout with debilitating depressive illness, I brought in a fraction of my usual income for the year. It's still clear that Brian and I have to get better at saving—but the difference between renting and owning is clear. Our home is more "ours," with equity that builds and we can tap into if we have to. For too long, our housing costs were a drain down which we flushed our money, never to be seen again. But there have also been times when a check from a family member arrived unannounced in the mail and paid a bill we weren't sure how we were going to pay.

Other than finding a faithful man, who will love her for the treasure that she is, this is what I want for Raina: a house, a home. She's already moved from temporary shelter to a partially subsidized two-bedroom apartment where she, her mother, a brother, her three young children, and one niece occasionally live. But most of us in this country are arrogantly ignorant of just how little it takes for a woman with children to end up homeless. Most people have no idea how it's possible to fall if you don't have a net to protect you.

When we Virginians imagine our homeless fellow citizens, do we factor in that about 40 percent of homeless people entering shelters have jobs? Until the birth of the twins, when Raina wasn't in school, she was working. Her mother, brothers, and sisters struggle financially, despite low-paying jobs. Do we know how wide a gap there is between rental costs and these so-called living wages—that the primary causes of homelessness are eviction, unemployment, low wages, and family crisis, not the personal and ethnic weaknesses that are more often given as reasons for people looking for shelter?

Making the transition off welfare is nearly impossible on a minimum-wage salary. According to NETWORK, a housing justice lobby, "the amount of available, affordable housing is so low that families across the country must earn an average of $13.57 an hour—more than *twice* the minimum wage—to afford a two-bedroom apartment at fair market rent." Another housing organization, Habitat for Humanity, reports: "The sad fact is that for each of the five million families now living in federally subsidized housing, there is another very-low-income family that is either homeless or precariously housed, or living in dilapidated housing or paying more than half their meager income for their homes. And there are four or five more low- or middle-income families with significant, though less-severe housing problems. And with the income gap widening, the stock of well-maintained affordable housing for low-income people is diminishing."

Raina and I both grew up in houses that contained our large families. Mine was a typical middle-class split-level kind of neighborhood on Long Island, where one lawn flowed into the next and the streets were quiet enough to play all those games my nieces would need a Secret Service escort to do now. Raina grew up in a house in rural Virginia close to relatives, growing up alongside her brothers and sisters. She, too, remembers the freedom of playing well outside the dimensions that defined her house and the land it stood on, the amazement that anyone would choose to stay indoors once the sun was up, and the joy of staying out until it was well below the horizon. We remember many of the same games, the picnic table as a permanent fixture of the backyard; the center of all water sports, the hose; the mystical sunset hours where secrets and horror stories were spilled; and chasing fireflies with mayonnaise jars carpeted with grass.

We always assumed that we'd stay in those childhood neighborhoods, in those familiar houses, but we didn't. We both wanted that oasis of childhood to pass on to our children. But in our early adolescence our families moved—not a matter of pleasure for our mother or siblings.

Now we are grown-ups. I live in a three-bedroom brick colonial that I "own." She lives in a locked, secure two-bedroom apartment, with a tiny kitchen, with too many people, smushed into a so-called garden apartment that abuts a parking lot where people treat the slow speed limits as suggested guidelines—leaving parents holding their breaths each time a kid gets close to the curb.

This is not what Raina wants for her children. But she is a single mother in a world that doesn't accord her the respect and the support that she deserves. She thanks God each time she makes it across the tightrope and prays for the net that will protect her and her children, that it break any fall that might hurt them. I want to be part of her net.

MOTHERHOOD BY PHONE

*I*t's 10:15 P.M. Raina is on the other end of the phone, the primary carrier of our friendship lately. She is worn, exhausted, and confused—pretty much what I'd expect of a single, working mother of three kids, age three and under living in a crowded two-bedroom apartment, with no car. But I haven't come close enough to what she's going through to be able to say

I've been there. Sometimes I wonder if that will always be a major block to a deeper friendship.

I have a husband with whom I've divided inside and outside work. We have a great deal of education that has allowed us higher paying jobs with benefits. We live in the cushion of the middle class, with extended families who could save us in a terrible financial crisis.

Motherhood exhaustion is a bit more familiar territory. That's a feeling I know. Having children is the highest vocation or mission for which I could ever have enthusiastically enlisted. But I also know what it costs—how it felt like sleep was a distant privilege of my youth, how the words "working" and "mother" went together far more easily on the page than they ever did in real life. Never mind *enlisting* in this noble endeavor for a couple of years. As a new mother, you can feel like you've been *drafted*—condemned to eternal boot camp with no perks or promotions in sight.

Raina has a strong faith in the calling of motherhood. She adores her kids and admires their feisty spirits. She feels instantly guilty when she complains and thinks she is being disloyal to say more. In contrast, I'm a firm believer that whatever natural frustration you get off your chest by talking, the less likely you are to find your feelings spilling into *unnatural* behavior. Raina is trying hard to break from the generations of mothers who used hitting as the first line of discipline, so she often feels like she's making it up as she goes along. And she has absolutely no idea what a good mother she is. But right now all she needs is an invitation to keep talking.

I take her on a stroll down my own rotten memory lane and share one of my many entries—locking myself in the bathroom, two-year-old Keara in meltdown right outside, the phone cord extending in from the kitchen and my friend Pat on the other end telling me that I was not in fact going to "lose it," that two-year-olds could try the patience of the saints on a good day, and that if it was around dinnertime, the use of alcohol (by me, not Keara) might be indicated.

Unfortunately, Raina's church prohibits the use of alcohol. Despite that, my example is a cruise on *The Love Boat* compared to everything she's got going; but something about my tale of woe encourages, less as comfort and more as invitation for her to keep talking.

I think of Simone Weil, a convert to Catholicism, an activist and writer who used to get totally overcommitted to whatever social justice program in which she was working. This would lead to a breakdown, in which her well-to-do parents would get her hospitalized until she pulled herself together enough to find some *other* project into which she could totally immerse herself. Her writing has a no-bullshit aspect to it that makes it accessible to me. "The love of our neighbor in all its fullness," Weil writes, "means being able to say to him, 'What are you going through?'" As simple and complicated as that. This brief admonition has helped me so much when I doubt that I can be "enough."

Raina tells a story—if you can call it that—since it doesn't have a specific beginning or end, just an interminable middle. She and the three kids were invited to a birthday party at a local park. To accomplish this she had to get three-year-old Jade and the twins bathed and dressed, which necessitated changing a huge blowout from one of the previously constipated boys immediately after he was dressed in an outfit matching his brother's.

She had to borrow her mother's car, trying to enlist Jade's help in keeping the twins on the sidewalk while she installed the infant seats in the back, taking forever to find working seat belts. Then she had to buckle two unhappy boys into their seats, barter with Jade about wearing a snug seat belt. Half-way out of the parking lot, she realized that she'd left the baby bag of diapers, premixed bottles, pacifiers, mats, blankets, and toys behind; she said a short prayer of thanks when she found it sitting on the sidewalk where she'd left it.

This entire preparation took five times as long as the ten-minute ride to the park. She shepherded the three kids and their stuff without even a stroller, which was especially difficult when two kids wanted to run ahead and the other demanded to be held. They were an hour late for the party. "I just got this crying feeling that kept building up inside," she explains.

"It was a simple birthday party but I had to keep telling Darren to slow down and stay right with me, when he should have been able to just run, but Deven was hanging on me and he started crying every time I tried to put him down. Jade was shy and uncomfortable in a new situation where the rest of the kids knew each other better than they knew her. I kept trying to get her out from behind my back and maybe play, but it took forever. Once they all started having a decent time, the party was over and I had to get three cranky, tired kids back to the car. Finally when they were all buckled in and sitting in the car, I started to cry.

"All I could feel was my aching back. I'm thinking ahead about dinner and baths and bedtime, doing it alone . . . alone . . . alone.

"I carried both boys and the bag in, with Jade whining and tugging on my shirt behind me. I couldn't get the door open fast enough. Then I put everyone and everything down on the floor and I couldn't help it — I started thinking about having to work tomorrow. . . . And, Martha, I just sat there crying. The kids stopped their whining and crying and whatever else they were doing and stared at me, all confused and worried. Jade smoothed my hair and went, 'Mommy, Mommy are you okay? Why are you crying, Mommy?' And all I could think of to say was 'Mommy's tired, Baby. Mommy's just real tired.' " Raina's crying now turns to a little laughter. "And you know what that child said to me?" She laughs and sniffles at the same time. "She said, 'Mommy, it's past your bedtime. You should go to bed right now.' "

"Wouldn't that have been interesting?" I add.

Raina is now laughing more than crying, but they're both there, capable of changing direction in a matter of seconds.

When I was a young mother, the unlimited energy I took for granted turned finite. Like with my car, I used to know about how far I could go after I filled up the tank. But motherhood requires high-octane fuel and burns it up so fast that I often ran on fumes. Even though I always wanted more than one child, I wondered where the extra energy would come from. Many mothers assured me that love automatically expands with each new child, which I had no trouble believing. It was always harder, however, to take it on faith that energy does the same thing.

It's after 11:00. Raina feels better for the talking, something she is coming to value in the grab bag of things that can make a person feel better. I try to give her as much encouragement as I can, while acknowledging that as a young mother I may have sometimes metaphorically skirted her general neighborhood but I was never ever *near* her wickedly difficult street.

Differences

*R*aina is my first black friend. And I am her first white friend. It's amazing in an area as racially diverse as the one where we live that the invisible racial lines regarding friendship are still so solid. Raina's never been too fond of white people. Her educational experience left her bitter about being overlooked and undervalued. In her early work experience with the school system, where she was a counselor in the after-school program, she felt the sting of fairly blatant racism from bosses. She hated receiving help from white people who were superficially kind but who expected a lot of bowing and scraping in return.

She never asked me for anything. Once I offered to baby-sit, and she took me up on it. I agonized over giving her money, not wanting to seem like the white savior. At the same time I knew that what was luxury money for me was just-getting-by money for her. The first time I gave her cash, I put it into an envelope and slipped it into her hand as she was leaving my house, like my father does surreptitiously on our birthdays, whispering, "Don't tell your mother."

I felt so self-conscious about money hurting our budding friendship that I finally asked her if it felt weird or insulting for me to give her cash. I was ready for some big heavy discussion. Instead, she laughed and told me that God has given me to her as a blessing and that whatever I shared with her was part of that blessing. It was a matter-of-fact statement of her strong faith: God answers your prayers through the people who come into your life.

I felt let off the hook by her perception that blessings come in all forms. The fact that I have some extra money right now is neither my fault or my glory. It's what I decide to do with it that matters. I don't want to *give* her money. I want to *share it* with her.

She said to me, "You're the only white person who's given me anything that I haven't felt 'less than' for taking."

I start to get the feeling that Raina is giving me something that I've had a hard time accepting from anyone except my family for the last few years. She and her children are pulling me out of my shell and out of my house. They are activating me, letting me feel my power by working on behalf of someone else as a precursor to feeling it for myself. Raina and her family are waking me up. They are calling to me to come out and play. And for the first time in too long a time, I want to go.

FATHER

*T*he children's father, James, was Raina's one and only, and he broke her heart. More than once. They planned to marry after the twins were born. They had found a little house well on the outskirts of the Washington, D.C., metropolitan area, with a decent rent. But when Raina discovered his infidelity she made a tough choice—to go it alone. James is by no means an involved father, although his kids love him, and I believe that he loves them. But most of the time, there's no "there" there.

Raina has to take him to court for financial support. Despite the fact that he doesn't live too far away, he rarely sees the kids. There's something likable about him. You want to see him grow up, get it together. He now has another young daughter, Jennifer. He lives with her and her mother.

I'd like to grab him by his collar and scream, "Your relationship with Raina is none of my business, but you are a fool to neglect these kids. They are just waiting for you to love them,

to be with them, you idiot. Grow the hell up, James. You will
live to regret your neglect. Your children feel the effects of your
neglect right now. And God help you with their futures."

But I don't.

BABY-SITTING

After adventures in baby-sitting at Raina's, and outings to
parks and fast-food restaurants, the kids start coming
over to our house. They are a hurricane, and with every move,
I see how far we have to go in the child-proofing area. We have
impromptu cookouts. I buy a cheapo baby pool at the crummy
drugstore down the street, some pails, and other water toys as a
surprise for one visit. Jade says, "You have a swimming pool!"
as if it's one of those fancy in-ground things that take up most
of peoples' yards. The boys can't be stripped down to their
Pampers fast enough. They have so much fun filling their pails
and dumping them out. It's nice to have them all contained
happily in a small place so Brian, Raina, and I can talk.

On indoor visits, while Jade colors or plays dress up, I find
the boys' love of water combines with their love of something
they can hardly pronounce: cooking. My kitchen floor could
always use a wash, so I sit them down on the floor and pull out
different sized bowls and all kinds of large plastic cooking im-
plements. It's clear they've watched Mom and Grandma make
dinner, because they are familiar with the tools. I can't wait to
cook with these guys. I predict to Brian that we are going to
spend a lot of time in the kitchen the next few years. The only
struggle is that they want to take all my cooking equipment (and
the water) home with them, and they are very unhappy when
they find that those things are not allowed in their baby bags.

After they've left, once we've cleaned up the significant trail the two little guys have left behind, Brian stops and faces me, "You know what, I haven't heard you laugh like that in a couple of years!"

"Really?" I ask.

"Oh yeah, I don't know what it is, but they bring something out in you that I haven't seen in a long while."

I don't exactly know what he means, but I do feel something I won't yet admit out loud: They take me out of myself. And that's a good thing. But it's not just me. I can see my husband falling in love with the children—a guy who ended up with one child, instead of the three or four he'd always expected. Raina's boys are totally different with a man. Maybe because their father is so minimally involved in their lives. They can sniff out testosterone a mile away. They roughhouse with him and call him gross, disgusting boy names, taunting and teasing him to chase them and punish them with upside down tickles. Brian is a child magnet. Kids see him and want to climb all over him. My nieces Tori and Gracie are just like that. "Oh, my little monkeys," he always calls them as he swings them around. The first time Darren and Deven started crawling all over Brian, they were giggling, he was laughing, and he automatically yelled out, "Oh, my little monk—guys," stopping himself from the same endearment that he uses with the children whose only difference happens to be that they're white. Somehow, with the twins, it seems wrong. It's strange. He never uses that particular endearment again.

When one of them is out of sight, I can usually find him sitting on Brian's lap as he works on the computer, or tracking him into the bathroom. Darren is particularly drawn to him. Brian shows his athletic prowess very early on. He gives, and then pulls back—not wanting to be perceived as trying to be their father.

"Oh, Brian, just be what you are," I tell him. "Be their friend. No one asked you to save them."

LITTLE BOYS

*R*aina decides to try to get into a regular habit with Jade—a girls' time-out to soothe her feeling of neglect that had set in shortly after the twins—definite crowd pleasers— came on the scene. I start baby-sitting for the twins when they're about eleven months old: headfuls of curly hair, round faces, limitless life. They don't look a thing alike, but they are wired together. Sitting in the midst of our living room, they'll end up crawling or toddling over the unfamiliar territory, speaking a language of two. It's hilarious. They take turns, they nod, their tone changes as they make points to each other.

Both are attached to identical pacifiers. When the boys are irritable, they automatically grab the two pacifiers and stick them into their unhappy mouths. I always wish I had a video camera each time they inevitably take a couple of sucks—make whatever determination they do at the same time—and then exchange the wrong pacifier for the right one. If they're close enough to each other, they actually stick the right pacifier into the other's mouth. No words, just this intricate exchange and, when successfully completed, kicking back to relax and enjoy the perfect pacifier.

They get nervous when their mom leaves them at my house. Lots of tears, with "Mama! Mama! Mama!"

She leaves. They stand at the closed door, tearful and be-wildered about who has just disappeared behind it.

They don't say much that I understand, but they comprehend a lot of what I say. There is nothing I can do to substitute for their mom. Two toddlers crying their eyes out is so hard. I can't even get their coats off. I pull the dining room chair up to the window and exclaim, "Look, look at the street!" (like it's the most interesting thing in the world). I try to pull something out of the hat from my experience of my niece Tori's early separation problems.

I live on a busy four-lane, divided street. At my worst with Tori, maybe just to drown out her wailing, I'd say, "Wanna watch traffic?" It didn't matter if it was hotter than hell or freezing cold, night or day, we would cuddle up and watch the cars and the cabs and the buses and trucks go by—a perfect tranquilizer. With the two boys I'm awkward managing them on the front steps, so I take the sport indoors. "Guys, wanna watch traffic?" They stand by the door sniffling and crying, looking like they're being held hostage. They take their pacifiers out now and then just so they can breathe.

"Oh look!" I say. "A big truck! *Vrrmm!*" I do this long enough to feel really stupid.

Finally Darren ventures forth and lets me lift him onto the chair. We pull the curtains aside, and he really starts getting into watching the traffic. Deven, slower to warm in all things, finally can't stand it anymore and decides to have a look. It works.

Several months into this habit, I'm cleaning the dining room. I get to tiny handprints all across the four windowpanes. I have window cleaner in one hand, paper towels in the other, but I love the pattern of those tiny fingers and I can't let them go. Not yet.

The boys also love the stairs. My blood pressure rises every time they go near them. Because they live in an apartment and everyone they know lives in apartments, they have no experience with a long flight of indoor stairs. Their ascent always has a climbing-Mount-Everest quality to it. The effort in those little legs is enormous. The descent however, drives me crazy. At first it's cautious backward crawling down, but that quickly graduates into bodysurfing. I don't recall child care being so involved and involving. I can't believe there are two more hours till nap time.

SCENES

When black adults are outside with white children or white adults with black children it creates an immediate social dissonance. You can almost see people trying to figure it out as they watch you chase the little kids down aisles or manage a tantrum because you've refused them a candy bar or try to keep six shoes tied, three noses cleaned, and three hats on. I always smile, thinking of the *Sesame Street* game where four objects are shown along with the song "One of these things is *not* like the others" and the task is to find the one that doesn't fit. Sometimes, I feel like the thing that's not like the others.

When three-year-old Jade, who is developing into quite the drama queen, is three seconds away from an all-out throw down because I won't buy her a sparkly pink Barbie camera in the drugstore that some idiot put up near the checkout, I have some harsh words for her. I pick her up and hold her horizontally against my hip. I'm fumbling with my purchases and credit card. She kicks and cries. The cashier, a middle-aged black woman, says to her, "Be good for your mama." Jade, who is quite socially attuned, starts screaming, "She's not

my mommy!" like I'm trying to kidnap her. I am so embarrassed and flustered that I throw the stuff into the bag and almost forget my credit card while struggling to manage the wild
child under my arm. I'm already wondering how to get her in
the car, not to mention strap her in the toddler seat. I can't believe one child can raise that much hell.

When we get to their apartment, Raina asks, "How did
it go?"

In a sign that I am feeling more comfortable with Raina, I
respond, "Picture this: shiny pink Barbie camera which Jade
falls in love with. Picture me saying no."

Raina starts to laugh in recognition of the storms that
sweet Jade can brew. I think she also gets a kick out of my seeing the inevitable dark side of her kids, not so much for what it
says about them but because of what it says about what *she*
must contend with some days.

"Okay," I say, feeling free enough to add to her pleasure.
"Now picture a black woman about your mom's age telling
Jade, 'Be good for your mama!' "

Raina is clutching her chest, she's laughing so hard.

"Welcome to the club," she tells me, as she laughs her ass off.

"Thanks . . . I think."

MOTHERS

*R*aina and I spend a lot of time talking about
motherhood—about the huge gap between what we
thought it would be and what it really is. The gap between the
job itself, "as advertised"—all pastels and twinkling sounds and
happy gurgling; sweet-smelling, reciprocal joy no matter what

the hour; love uncompromised by sleep deprivation, an extra fifteen pounds, an awe verging on panic at the length of the commitment. We talk about ourselves as mothers—especially the waves of anger, loneliness, not liking who we are with our kids. In our minds we know that we can never be "enough," yet forget it each day our children make it clear that we are missing the mark.

Before you become a mother and then after—maybe for a little while, when things are going well—you might actually convince yourself that for every problem, there is a solution. And if you can just find it and then do it, you will prevail. This is not some illusion that sets in with the hormones of pregnancy. It's a combination of the wish to manage things while living in a culture that has given mothers the weight of considerable responsibility and control—with almost no power. There are experts, books, and every possible form of input that lead to putting the big *ing* in parenting; moving it from a role—"who you are"—to a series of tasks and activities—"what you do." And while most of the books admit to no simple answers, they deliver an implicit message that knowledge and understanding are central to "good parenting." These fonts of wisdom offer standards by which we can assess our own kids from the physical, which is the most measurable, to the psychological, with such ephemeral but demanding concepts as self-esteem.

But how do you *really* know you're a good mother?

Raina and I haven't a clue.

A STEP FURTHER

*T*ill now, Raina and I get to know each other at each end of the child exchange. When she drops them off at our place, we "visit" mostly about the kids—hers and mine. On one level, I can't wait to see her lit headlights as she pulls up in front of my house to collect them. The kids exhaust me. However, this is the time Raina is at her most relaxed. The kids love staying on while their mom is here. And Raina seems to love to just kick back with a soda.

Somehow, threaded in and out of our observations of the kids' antics or our bitching about the things that keep getting in our way, we begin talking about ourselves. Our backgrounds, the families we grew up with—without the whitewash. She tells me about her estrangement from her father and the impact it's had on her relationship with men. I describe my father's drinking, how I prayed and prayed as a child that he would stop. How my relationship with him changed so dramatically in my twenties when he quit and stayed totally alcohol free. We lament a sorry similarity—drugs that have delivered their poison to our siblings, the years of struggles that our brothers and sisters have had, and the miracle that they are all now clean and sober. Our mothers are strong—a source of pride, support, and the occasional irritation that comes with women so certain of themselves.

We begin to share our own kinks—the things that embarrass us, like the fact that we both struggle with driving phobias the major concern of which is getting lost. Somehow introducing some personal weakness makes us more attached to each other. It also makes us laugh.

Raina articulates something on my mind. "You're so easy to talk to."

"I was just thinking that about you," I tell her. "I don't find it all that easy to shoot the breeze with people I don't know too well."

"But I thought you did," she says.

"Why?"

"Just overhearing you talk on the phone to your sisters or cousins or mother."

"Between your family and mine, that's only about half the universe."

She's a great audience. She thinks I'm funny. As we try to carry on "normal conversation," we are constantly interrupted by the needs of the kids. Jade runs in with a desperate report of the twins' misbehavior. Raina patiently resolves the problem.

Once Jade is out of earshot, I impulsively say, "I think it's time for a girls' time-out. I mean, I hate shopping, but do you want to go out for lunch? The kids will be at Our Lady Queen of Peace Early Childhood Learning Center . . . so we'd have no interruptions." I immediately feel self-conscious. Is what we have right now all she wants and no more? Is going out to lunch a financial conflict? Since it's my idea, I want her to know that it's my treat, but I don't know how to tell her without insulting her. Her hesitation is making me uncomfortable.

"Great," she then says with surprising enthusiasm. "I'm pretty sure I have a coupon for the Olive Garden and my cousin might still be working there."

"I thought I had a lot of cousins—"

"You never know when it might help out."

"Good, let's go there. You set the date," I tell her.

"Next Wednesday," she decides. "Can you drive?"

"You know how I am—as long as it's not too far away, it's fine."

"Okay, then pick me up at twelve-thirty."

"What will we talk about without the kids?" I tease.

"I don't know, Martha. Somehow I don't think that's gonna be a problem."

"No, I don't either."

When I pick her up, I tell her she looks so different.

"You're right," she agrees. "I don't have a child on me." But it's more than that. Her hair is pulled back. She's wearing make-up and earrings. She has an almost regal bearing. I'm struck by what a beautiful woman she is.

"You look nice with makeup on," she tells me.

"Well, don't get used to it. One of the big reliefs of not having to get up and go into the office every day is no more make-up, blow-drying hair, wearing stockings, and the dry-cleaned dresses."

"So you've given all that up?" she asks.

"Well, I think we can safely say that I've cut down on it quite a bit."

She laughs at the unfortunate truth of what I'm saying — which is that I've become a slob. "But you look really good today."

"Thanks. As my mother would say, 'I made an effort.' "

The Olive Garden is fairly close and surprisingly not too crowded. Once in the restaurant, her smile disappears. I've seen it happen before, in stores and other service places. She gets ready to be stern, if need be — strange because she's such a gentle person. The hostess seats us immediately at a table in the midst of a number of banquettes. Raina's neck gets stiff and she says very seriously, "Excuse me, but can we have the corner booth?" indicating the empty one.

The young hostess consults her clipboard as if it contains State Department blueprints and finally says, "Of course. Follow me." Raina nods, follows, and surveys the booth. We sit down and Raina lights up again, all smiles.

The waiter has to come back four times before we can shut our mouths long enough to master the formidable menus and come up with an order. She gives the waiter the coupon for lunch ahead of time, just to make sure everything's in order. She asks for her cousin Krysta, not knowing whether she's working today or not.

Krysta, working in another part of the restaurant, comes by. "Hey, girl, how you been?" she says, hugging Raina.

"Fine, fine. This is my girlfriend Martha."

"Hey, Martha."

Krysta is not one to hold back. "How do you two know each other?"

Raina and I haven't really worked that one out. "We're neighbors," I say. This seems perfectly plausible to Krysta, but it makes me uncomfortable and I know it does Raina, too.

Krysta winks and says, "Don't order dessert. I'm gonna bring you something."

"What did I tell you?" Raina smiles.

"Just what I need—more pounds."

"I know. I still have to take this weight off from the twins."

"Yeah. Me, too," I say.

"Guess you're taking it real slow," she responds, given the fact that my last pregnancy was over twenty years ago.

I'm not sure I want to get into this, but if she's going to know me . . . well, she has to know it all. "Actually, the weight's not really from Keara. I mean there's a few pounds that have never left me, but I was one forty, played racquetball three times a week, did aerobics a couple of times a week, walked."

The surprise on her face is a pretty accurate reflection of how I feel when I look in the mirror. "What happened?" she asks.

"You know how I told you that I've had some trouble with depression?"

"Yeah."

"Well, it's worse than that. I've had terrible trouble with depression. Bad enough for years of medicines that all have weight gain as a side effect, bad enough for me to go into Arlington Hospital for a few weeks, bad enough to have electroconvulsive therapy."

"What's that?" she asks.

"It's shock therapy. Not as bad as it sounds. It brought me back."

I can see her wondering what I have to be depressed about.

"The worst thing about the kind of depression I have is that it comes and goes, often not connected to anything in my life. Let's face it, I have a great life. But the kind of depression I have flattens me. Or I'm so agitated I don't sleep, I can't sit still. It's hell on earth."

"Why haven't you told me?"

"I don't know. I guess . . . well, I guess I was worried what you'd think of me. How comfortable you'd be leaving the kids with me. . . . Just . . ." I'm getting hoarse, and the tears I'm trying to hold back are stinging the hell out of my eyes so I can hardly see. One drops on the bread plate. Then another. It becomes clear that there is no leak in the ceiling. I am crying. "I'm sorry."

"Martha, what are you sorry for?"

"For crying. You have so much to deal with and here I am with no one to take care of but myself with work I can do at home."

She angrily waves away the apology. "Y'know I whine to you all the time."

"Raina, the whole time I've known you I have never heard you whine."

"Well, I feel like I do. And I've known you carry burdens you don't talk about."

"I never know what people who didn't know me before will think."

"I'm sorry that you've had such hard times," she says.

Before I can disagree or compare our woes, she grabs my hand and squeezes it. I squeeze back. Something has shifted. I have needed her and, in spite of myself, have let her know it. For me, she was what I hope I am for her: there.

ENTITLEMENTS

I was raised to be grateful: to see the good things in life as blessings from God and — a stretch — to accept bad things as hidden blessings. I was raised to say thank you, to expect others to do for me only that which I couldn't do for myself. I was discouraged about making proclamations concerning what I deserved or didn't deserve. To my chronic complaint, "That's not fair!" my mother stated the obvious but difficult to swallow truth, "Life's not fair." This is a woman who, when accused of punishing any of us when it turned out we weren't guilty of the particular offense, shrugged off sending us to our room, taking away dessert, or giving us extra chores with the suggestion to "just apply it to something you did and didn't get caught for."

But while I was being programmed for gratitude, I was quietly coached in the art of entitlement. I was entitled to have my hard work translated into recognition and some success. I learned the bag of tricks for greasing the wheels of the system —

politely, respectfully, but firmly. An old ad echoes from my childhood: "Accept nothing less." The old adage "If at first you don't succeed, try, try again" was communicated almost as a promise. But to Raina, "If at first you don't succeed . . ." is often a prediction, and a negative one at that. If at first you don't succeed . . . it's pretty good evidence that you won't in the future.

Raina is not a passive person and I am no steamroller. I have to work up a head of steam to push for my rights. It's easier to push for the rights of other people than my own. But it's a matter of execution, not intention. In many ways, Raina is much more assertive than I. But Raina sees brick walls where I see open doors. It's in the puffing up, the bullshitting, the network of people I know or can be called upon, and the absolute conviction that I'm not asking for one iota more than what my family or I deserve.

The problem is that when you don't have much money and you have young kids, you are in the constant position of having to speak up to people at places where your voice can be so easily muted or silenced altogether. As I learn more about Medicaid, food stamps, child care subsidies, and Social Security, I have to laugh when I hear these things being called "entitlements," like they're special, extra. As Americans and as humans, food, shelter, and health care should be rights—not gifts given and taken back at the whim of whatever social policies are in vogue at the time.

What's Wrong with This Picture?

I remember a spot on the TV evening news from when I was a child about how a number of congressional wives

and their families were going on a welfare diet. They would be as-
signed the appropriate amount of food stamps and other cash for
which they would qualify, based on the number of people in their
families. The program showed the families, most of whom had
Olympic smiles at the beginning of the weeklong adventure—
giving quotes like they were going off on a camping trip.

In a report several days later, there was a little grousing
when one of the adolescent girls learned that food stamps
wouldn't cover her particular brand of soap. The women were
just as pleased as punch with themselves when pictured leaving
the store, having stayed within their budgets. Two days later,
the kids bitched and moaned about the boring food, the sacrifice of food lunches, money for Cokes, Twinkies, and even Juicy
Fruit gum.

The women admitted more freely the challenge of making
interesting food to please their discriminating (complaining)
families. From the look of the manicures on some of them, the
expensive suits with the matching hats, and the way they
moved around, unpacking their bags and opening cabinets and
drawers, I wondered if some of those women actually knew the
way to their own kitchens.

The upshot of the whole story at the end of the week was
that, "yes," the congressional families admitted, "it could get
boring." But the women emphasized that it wasn't *all that hard*
to turn out nutritious, satisfying, and filling meals with food
stamps and financial limits. The implication was, So what's the
problem with all those welfare mothers?

I remember the whole thing pissed me off—puzzling because
at the time my deepest concern in life was that my mother
would allow me to wear the lightest of pink lipsticks. The only
social justice that generally interested me was my own.

The congressional food challenge came back to me over the

years. I remembered it when I worked and lived in an "economically challenged" rural drug rehabilitation program, where we faced the constant challenge of feeding residents within similar financial constraints. In the middle of the fifth boxed macaroni-and-cheese dinner in two weeks, it finally came to me why the congressional-wives-versus-the-welfare-mothers project had annoyed me as it had.

It was never a fair fight.

It takes so much more than a week's worth of cash and coupons to feed a family: a car, gas, a newspaper for coupons and comparing prices, enough money to save money by shopping in bulk, kitchen appliances—like a working refrigerator to store fresh fruits and vegetables, meats and dairy. A freezer to keep cooked-ahead meals or to take advantage of sales, decent hot and cold running water—in short, a working kitchen. For many of the working poor, trying to make it on the minimum wage, perhaps with multiple jobs, just the time and energy to shop, cook, and put together three meals doesn't often feel as much a right as a luxury.

That was the seed that took root in my restless, shallow preadolescence. The idea could not germinate and grow without very real exposure, experience, and oppression at the never endingness of it as I shared responsibility for keeping kids full when our pockets were always close to empty.

Hunger is not an experiment. It's a day in, day out curse, one that's going to take a whole lot more than adding a few bucks to food stamps every month.

AUNTS AND AUNTIES

*A*t some point in the relationship between adults and children, there comes the question of how the adults should be addressed. In my family, we've been casual, our children calling their aunts and uncles by their first names, which is curious, since we wouldn't dare call our own aunts and uncles by theirs. My sister Rachel has her kids call their neighbors Mr. or Miss with their first names—which seems to work. I don't see myself as a "Miss Martha" to anyone. This question resolves itself one day when I'm with Raina's kids and a cashier refers to me as the children's grandmother. One of them pipes up and protests, "She's not our grandmother. She's our aunt." Of course, people are actually no more enlightened about our relationship than they were before.

There's "aunt" and there's "auntie." Raina's sisters are Auntie Alana and Auntie Kendra. I am plain aunt, and Brian is uncle. And it cracks me up that the kids somehow made the distinction.

People in our two families begin to meet one another. On his way to meet my sister Rachel's new baby, Sean, Darren yells out from the backseat with great enthusiasm, *"Sean the baptist?"*

I start getting to know Elizabeth, Raina's mother—a teacher's aide at a local elementary school. She is an incredible cook who bakes as if she believes the cholesterol warnings are vastly overstated. At first, I thought she was terrible with vegetables; her spinach was disgusting. Everyone got a big laugh once I discovered that the spinach was actually "greens." She tried holding out her sweet potato pie until I ate all my greens, but took pity on me after Brian and Raina told numerous stories about my narrow eating preferences.

Brian reminisces about the first time I had breakfast with his family. There was this white stuff on the plate, which I assumed at first glance was cottage cheese. Everything else—the fried eggs, the bacon, sausage patties—was swimming in grease, so I went for the white stuff. Bad choice. I had to spit it out in my napkin. It turns out this was my introduction to grits. Of course, after Brian tells the story, Elizabeth insists she can whip up some grits I would like. I assure her that it would be physically impossible. People who have their roots in the South eat some strange foods. Brian's mother and Raina's mother seem to put parts of pigs in all kinds of strange places . . . like vegetables. They believe in cooking vegetables until they surrender their color and their ability to stand up for themselves. On the plus side, I've discovered that the chicken my mother always called fried was not even of the same species as the stuff my mother-in-law and Elizabeth cook up.

SLEEP OVER

Technically, the kids have slept at our house many times, but always as a result of extensions of child care. They fall asleep in spite of themselves while waiting for their mom. Sometimes we let them stay rather than wake them up for the arduous ritual of leaving—complete with coats; hats; boots; collecting their stuff, including pacifiers that could be anywhere, bottles, favorite blankies. And as hard as it is to pull off at our place, with Brian, Raina, and me working together, the prospect of Raina having to take care of it all at the other end is just too much. She usually heads home, sets the alarm for early morning, so the kids don't wake up with all of their internal alarms going wild, trying to understand their obvious abandonment.

Jade is the first to sleep over as a fun activity done on purpose. She arrives, with three pink-and-purple bags overflowing with toys and hopefully pajamas and a change of clothes. She is spilling over with excitement and has a mental menu that is impossible to fit into a sixteen-hour period, but I'm not about to tell her now. "I love being here"—she beams, then emphasizes—"alone." A Happy Meal at McDonald's, a trip to the video store with plans to get three videos—which I talk down to two. I had promised at one time to take her to the local bookstore. Unfortunately she has a steel-trap memory and decides that now is the time to call the marker in. Later, she inspects Keara's old room and unpacks her stuff. Keara's room is Girl Wonderland to Jade. She checks out the high bed with a bit of trepidation but then settles in with the pillows and quilt, uses the Kleenex box next to the bed for no reason, flips the bedside lamp off and on. From the perspective of the bed, she can see some of Keara's old Barbies, stuffed animals, and huge book collection. She leans back in total comfort and sighs, "Keara is so lucky."

"Yeah, she is," I tell her, so aware that, as an only child, Keara was truly the center of our universe. Maybe, with the way it hurts so much to have her far away, she was too important, too indulged, too much the recipient of her father's and my singular attention. I have no idea. Jade is thrilled when I point out her own towel and washcloth and a little basket I filled for her from our huge stash of hotel freebies—soaps, shampoos, emery boards, etcetera. Okay, I went overboard. I am so thrilled to have a little girl sleeping over.

"Aunt Martha, there's just one thing," she says very seriously. "My mom said not to touch my hair."

"Why not?"

"She said you can't handle it."

"What do you mean, I can't handle it?"

"Remember the last time you did my hair?"

"It looked pretty good."

"My mom said it was a disaster."

"What did I do to your hair?"

"Remember how you used that jelly stuff to smooth it all down?"

"Yeah. It didn't work out?"

"No, it was bad."

"Oh well, you know I'm used to my hair and Keara's hair. I guess I have to learn about your hair."

"Yeah, 'cause I have much more hair than you. And it's thick. And my mom can make it look all different ways, and yours is just that one way."

"Yeah, you and your mom have hair like each other, and Keara and I have the same kind of hair."

"So I'll take a bath in the morning, but you won't do my hair."

"I promise I won't touch your hair."

"Okay, now what are we gonna do?"

We cook, we read, we do arts and crafts, we fool around with the computer, we play dress up. I keep trying to get her interested in television, because I am so damn tired.

Brian's working late, so we order in pizza. In perfect luxury, we consume it on Brian's and my bed, gulping down our drinks and watching *The Wizard of Oz* on the VCR. About halfway through, her eyelids have trouble staying in the up position. Each time I suggest she's tired, she denies it with great indignation. When she starts snoring, I'm on firmer ground. "C'mon, Jade, let's get you into bed." I help her into Keara's bed and tuck her in.

Through her sleep, she whispers, "Tell Uncle Brian he has to kiss me good night."

"Okay."

"Even if I'm really asleep, tell him to kiss me good night."

When I promise I will, she sighs, turns over, and lets herself fall into a deep and satisfying sleep. She's not even aware of Brian's kiss later that night, although she insists she remembers it over a totally nonnutritive cereal and Dunkin' Donuts Munchkins the next morning, while I inhale the largest coffee they make.

Since Keara left, since Tori decided our house was permanently contaminated by the *Beauty and the Beast* sequel, it's been too long since a little girl has slept in that bed. I can't explain the happiness. I feel full.

MAKING CHANGE AT THE 7-ELEVEN

*R*aina calls to see if I want to look at a used car she's thinking of buying. She heard about it from a friend. It's at some gas station, which between the two of us will take forever to find. But it's a gorgeous day and I'm sick of sitting, chained to my computer, scrambling words to make them read better. In the meantime, she borrows her mother's big car, which itself is close to biting the dust. Raina's got her favorite gospel music blaring. The kids are happily buckled in the backseat. It's a roll-down-the-windows-and-inhale-the-promise-of-spring kind of day. We cruise down Columbia Pike, all of us singing. I can't believe I'm starting to like and remember gospel music. I've got my feet propped up against the dashboard. I've got an afternoon to kill, and I feel twenty years younger.

The kids have the same spunk that I feel.

"What are we doing?"

"Can we do something fun?"

"Aunt Martha, can we sleep over?"

"Can we go to McDonald's?"

"Can we get candy?"

I'm dying to catch up with Raina's news of the week. "I say we think of them as background music," I suggest.

"You!" She laughs like I've said something outrageous.

The kids have no intention of leaving us alone.

"All right, we'll stop at the 7-Eleven right after we see the car," I offer, "my treat."

"Do you *promise*?" demands Jade.

"Yes, yes, yes!"

We pull into a gas station that could only be described as marginal. There isn't a single car on the lot that approaches normality.

The Pakistani owner looks at us like we are questionable customers — I have no idea why.

He points to a car that looks like it has seen military action . . . and lost. It is a bomb. "I know the gentleman who own this car and he only drive back and forth from gas station."

"Yeah," I whisper to Raina, "fifty times a day for fifty years."

He sets the price at $600.

I laugh out loud.

Raina gives me a look.

"No way. This car is worth half that," I insist.

He acts like I've insulted his mother.

Raina gently shoves me aside, where I should have been all along. "Could you please pop the hood?" she asks.

"Pop the hood?" I'm looking at her like, *Where did you get that?*

She looks up and down the entire engine. I know for a fact that she doesn't have a clue what she's looking at, but she makes

a great show of it and that's all that matters. She pulls me aside
for a consultation. We spend a few minutes talking seriously,
with nodding and gestures, about the merits of Pepsi versus
Coke or something else we actually know something about.

"I think we need to take it for a test drive."

"Well, go ahead. I'll wait here with the kids."

"Yeah, that would be a lot easier."

The owner looks a little uncomfortable when she requests
the keys. Like a prospective buyer wouldn't want a test drive?
She surely isn't driving off with no plans to return, especially
leaving her young children and big-mouth friend behind (although I must say, she takes off alone with a certain zest that
gives me a moment's pause).

Deven has a fit, as if she's taken off for good. I have to hold
him tight and whisper promises of sugar in his ear.

Darren and Jade seem fairly certain that she'll come back,
but the unfulfilled desire for Slurpees grows by the minute.

Within five minutes, Raina pulls in with furrowed brow
and slight frown indicating that something is wrong with the
car. She tells the owner that she has to find out when "some
guys" who "know cars" can come to check it out.

Thinking about summer coming, I suggest she check the
air conditioner. Nothing. She checks the heat. Nothing. At all.

The gas station guy feigns total surprise. Raina figures that
with spring coming, if the car checks out in other ways, she can
do without the heat and maybe get the air-conditioning fixed
later. Either way, if she can get that car for $350 to $400, even if
she uses it only for six months, it's worth it. She tells him, con-
ditional on her brother's opinion, she'll give him $350. He says,
"four hundred." They strike a deal. Brian and I have already
pledged $250 toward a car. If she clears out her bank account,
she'll just make it. Having her own wheels will be priceless.

After waiting, albeit impatiently, during our car negotia-
tions, the kids are now in overdrive, clamoring for 7-Eleven.
Once there, Raina buys a loaf of bread and exits. The Slurpee
choices go easily enough, but the candy . . . my God, I had no
idea there was so much. An entire aisle of it. The decision making is interminable. Once they see what the others have chosen,
they become less certain about their picks. I finally have to
count down from twenty or we'll never leave. The kids deposit
their stuff on the counter next to their Slurpees. It's only when
I start to pay that I realize I'm wearing my old purple sweatpants that seem to have no pockets and no wallet. "Okay, no
problem" I tell the cashier. I begin deep-sea diving into my very
large bag. The kids reach for their haul, but the guy stops me
from handing out the goodies, holding them hostage until I
fork over the cash.

"I beg your pardon," I say, laying on an offended voice a little thick with sarcasm . . . but it's insulting.

I reach down, grab handfuls of change, and dump them out
on the counter. Then I start stacking by quarters and dimes,
with the guy watching every count I make like I'm trying to
cheat him. To make it just that much better, the coins from the
very bottom are mixed in with peanut-butter-cracker crumbs,
paper clips, and New York City cab receipts, plus an earring
I'd given up all hope of finding. With all the noise the impatient
kids are making, I look for Raina. She's standing outside,
watching as if she doesn't know us. I get distracted by the kids
and the rather unhappy look from the cashier, so I make piles
of smaller denomination coins. I'm down to nickels, then the
dreaded pennies. I can tell this guy hates my guts, even though
no one is waiting behind me. When you start paying for things
with small change, people act like you're trying to get away
with something.

"Aunt Martha, I want my Slurpee," whines Darren.

Jade chimes in, "Why can't we have our candy?"

"The man won't let us have it till I give him all the money," I say tightly.

"Then why don't you just give him the money?"

"Well, I forgot my wallet—but don't worry, I have leftover money."

"So, get it," Deven, still hanging on my hip, proposes this like he's just come up with the most original of solutions.

"Will you let me concentrate? C'mon, you guys. I have to count."

Jade rushes up to help with her own brand of kindergarten counting and messes with the piles, which only screws up the process more.

It's a squeaker, but after fumbling into every zippered and snapped corner and pocket of my bag, we've got at least nineteen cents to spare. The guy collects the piles of coins like I've deposited turds on his counter. I give him an exaggerated and slightly sarcastic, "Thank you so very much," grab the goodies, and collect the kids.

As we get in the car, Raina looks at me and shakes her head.

"What's the matter?" I ask.

She is half amused and half horrified. "I can't believe you just did that!"

"Well, these are my old sweats and I guess my money must be in another pair."

"Oh, I can believe you forgot your money. I can't believe you stood there and paid with all that change. . . . I can't believe he let you."

"*Let me,*" I sputter, feeling the mighty power of WASPdom— even though technically I don't qualify because of the Catholic part, and I may not have the Anglo-Saxon either—but I was feeling that Great Entitlement that white people whose families have been in the country for a long time often learn to feel.

"*Let* me?" I repeat. "What choice did he have? It's real money and it's too damn bad if it made him work a little harder."

Then I apologize in front of the kids for using a swear word, which I keep reminding myself is unacceptable in Raina's family.

"Look at what you're wearing." She points to my clothes. My pink, hooded sweatshirt is well-worn. My purple sweatpants have admittedly seen better days. They're a bit thin in the seat, not to the point of passing daylight through them, but just about. My hair looks sort of bad because it hasn't been washed in a couple of days, and it hasn't been colored in many more. For purposes of convenience I've pulled it back with a hairband, which is really more of a ski band. I have no makeup on. My socks match, but they are red, and my running shoes are at least ten years old. It's my typical writing and running around the neighborhood gear. I hear echoes of Keara's "Have you no pride?" when I've gone out like this.

I glance over and notice that Raina looks a lot better that I do. Her hair is tightly pulled back in a bun. She's not wearing much makeup, but she never seems to need it as much as I do. She has on a sweatshirt and pants, but they're newer and they match. Come to think of it, her kids look a lot better than I do, too.

"Raina," I protest, "you told me you were coming right over. I didn't have time to change."

She rolls her eyes. "Martha, I could have given you an hour and would you have changed?"

"Probably not," I admit. "I would have kept working till the minute you showed up."

She continues to shake her head and laugh.

I realize that I walk through the world with such different expectations than she does. Raina tells me that anytime she's come close to doing what I just did, she has felt so suspected, so harassed, that she's left the store.

"My money is as good when I look like this as when I'm in a five-hundred-dollar suit," I pontificate, "and woe to the cashier who doesn't know that."

"You're a mess!" She laughs, and doesn't stop laughing the whole way home.

SLEEPING ARRANGEMENTS

Now that they've turned three, the boys have graduated to purposeful sleep overs. I explain my distaste for bringing unhappy children home to their mothers in the middle of the night, and they explain to me that they are not children, they are big boys. They pack as if headed for a monthlong expedition. Raina points out the real bag, the one with clothes and supplies. They've packed the rest themselves: pillows, blankets, toys, some cans of baked beans, and a box of cereal. I would love to have seen this process.

Darren knows all about how kids sleep over in Keara's room. He looks with trepidation at the height of Keara's bed and decides to settle in on the floor. They adore our flashlights, so I bought them each one from the dollar store to use in addition to the night-light in Keara's room. Darren is active— exploring Keara's room, choosing stuffed animals he might want to sleep with, books he might want to read in bed.

"Deven," he calls, "I have a idea. Let's pretend . . ." And I know he is well on his way into those constructions of imagination that let loose when you are in a different place. Uncharacteristically Deven wants no part of this game. He has clear plans of his own.

Brian comes home at dinnertime—early for him. I notice that when he mounts the stairs to change into more comfortable clothes, Deven is right behind. He follows Brian into the bedroom and stops at our bed. At some point, Deven has slipped his blanket, pillow, and favorite stuffed animal onto Brian's side of the bed.

Deven stands silently, his hands on his hips, waiting for Brian's reaction.

"Is this your stuff?" Brian asks.

"Yeah," Deven replies. "Where are *you* gonna sleep?"

WHAT AM I? WHAT WILL I BE?

*D*arren, Deven, and Jade sit with Brian and me over dinner in one of our delightfully circuitous conversations that challenges the length of the candles. We talk about what we want to be when we grow up. Jade knows immediately. "When I grow up I'm going to be a scientist . . . and a teacher." Darren, perplexed by the question, remains silent. Deven has a different take on the question. "Before I was a little boy, I was a businessman and I had a car and a apartment. And I had a girlfriend. Her name was Cynthia."

Darren is still clearly stumped. "It's okay," Brian tells him. "When I was your age I wasn't sure what I wanted to be."

"I know something," Darren offers, slightly changing the direction of the conversation. "We're supposed to be black and you're supposed to be white, but that's not right."

"How's it wrong?" I ask.

"Just look at my face." He juts out his face for a good look. "I'm not black. I'm brown. Light brown."

"Like your mom," Brian offers.

Deven jumps in. "No, our mom's white."

"No," replies an exasperated Jade. "She's light brown."

"Uh-uh," Darren insists. "Just ask her. She's white."

"And what about *me*?" I ask.

"You're pink, not white," he counters. "Now, *Keara's* white."

"Uncle Brian has *some* white, but his nose and cheeks are red," Deven adds.

"Who cares?" Jade complains.

It's clear that the boys still do.

"A lot of people used to care *a lot*," I say.

"Why?" Darren demands.

"Remember that book I got you last year about the little girl Ruby Bridges?"

"Yeah, yeah, I do," yell Darren and Jade.

"I *love* that story," Darren says with relish. "Y'know what I remember?" he continues. "The part where she was going to school and there were these people yelling and some men had guns and I didn't know if they were gonna shoot her, but you said they were police guys who weren't letting anyone get in the way of her getting in the school."

"Right," I say, "and you know what *I* remember about the first time I read it to *you*?"

"What?"

"You looked and looked really hard at the faces of the grown-ups and you couldn't believe how mean they looked. Jade and Deven were finished with the page. They wanted me to keep reading, but you wanted to see every single part of those two pages."

Deven is struggling. "I still don't get it. Is it a real story or is it not true?"

"It's true," I tell him.

Darren attempts to fill in the blanks. "This little girl wanted to go to a school where only white children were allowed to drink water."

"No, *Darren,*" Jade interrupts. "She wasn't allowed to go to the school where white kids went."

"No, Jade, there was *two* water fountains and kids got in trouble if they got water out of the wrong one," Darren corrects her.

"You're *both* right." I mediate. "Black people and white people didn't do things together. White people wanted to be the bosses of everything. If a black boy drank from a white fountain, he'd get in a lot of trouble. White kids and black kids weren't allowed to play together or go to school together, and white schools got better stuff than black schools."

"Why?"

"A long, long time ago black people were taken from their homes in Africa and brought to this country, even though they didn't want to, and they were made into slaves."

"Oh! Oh! I know about slaves." Jade raises her hand like she's in school. "White people owned black people and they were mean to them."

Brian and I look up at each other, wondering if we can deflect the inevitable. "How about more spaghetti?" he asks brightly.

"You can't *own* somebody," Darren says like it's the silliest thing he's ever heard.

"No, you can't," I agree. "It was very wrong . . . but a lot of people wanted it, so it took a long time to change. And Ruby, the girl in the book, made a big change that helped. She went to a school where there were only white kids. And the white people were really mad. And do you remember what Ruby did?"

"Yeah, yeah." Jade remembers. "She just went right in anyway."

"That's right."

"And . . . and she said prayers," Jade adds proudly.

"Sweetie, you have such a good memory!" I tell her.

"And Darren and Deven, too!" Brian adds, heading off a compliment showdown.

I'm relieved to be finished with this discussion. I try to introduce an issue where the most controversial question is who will be allowed to make the first cut in the cake.

Darren is still unsettled. "But what were those grown-ups screaming at Ruby?"

I still remember his fascination with the detailed illustration by George Ford of tiny Ruby challenged by angry crowds surrounded as she tried to enter the school on the first day.

"They were saying, 'Go home,' " I suggest.

"No," he disagreed. "They said, 'We hate you.' "

"It was mean," I agree.

"Is that why the men with guns were around her?"

"Yes," I answer. "To protect her from getting hurt."

"Yeah, but why didn't they have police clothes on?"

"They're a special kind of police called FBI agents. My dad was an FBI agent," I tell them.

Deven perks up. "Was he in the book?"

"No. He was probably helping someone else that day."

"Did he have a gun?" asks Deven.

"Yes, but whenever he came home, even before he said hello to us, he went upstairs and locked it in a drawer in his bedroom."

"Grandfather John?" Jade asks, surprised—she's met my dad.

"Yes. That was his job. Now, who wants dessert?"

"Me!"

"Me!"

"Me!"

"It's my turn to cut," claims Jade.

"Uh-uh, it's mine," says Darren.

"You can each cut your own piece, but if you start fighting I'll cut everybody's piece ... and they'll be really small," I threaten.

Then we have the inevitable discussion of who gets corners versus middles. Luckily the cake is large enough to oblige all wishes.

It's Darren's turn to accompany me at the sink, scraping dishes and washing the pots and pans. Brian and the other kids have drifted off to the family room.

I'm exhausted by dinner.

Darren is uncharacteristically quiet. A few minutes later he turns to me. "I know what I want to be when I grow up."

"What?" I ask expectantly.

He stares out the kitchen window as he gives his answer. "A stranger," he says quietly but decisively. "I'm gonna be a stranger."

THE STORIES

It gives me such joy to see Brian, Raina, and the kids forge their own relationship, apart from me. It took a long time for Brian to let go of his protectiveness of me, the fear that I would be inundated by becoming overly involved. His real fear, of course, is that any change in my life will make me vulnerable to hyperness followed by crushing depression. Exhaustion and little kids go hand in hand, and it has taken time to see that I'm up for it, that I'm having fun.

His initial reaction when he walks through the door at 9:30 after a very long day at work to find us playing in the living room, stereo screaming, toys littering the floor, dinner dishes still on the table, and Raina and me shooting the breeze on the couch with our legs propped up on the coffee table, is the Look. It is disapproval, unhappiness. It says, *This is supposed to be our quiet time together.* But then he gets three kids running and wrapping themselves around his knees with an enthusiasm usually reserved for well-known athletes or actors. Testosterone is in the house, and each child has something special they want from him. The boys just want contact. He picks them up, swings them over his shoulder, carries them on his back. They want him to scare them, chase them, wrestle them to the ground.

Raina notices the heavy briefcase and the tired shoulders. As he leans over and kisses her hello, she empathizes. "I bet you're surprised."

"A little," he agrees as he leans over and kisses me.

Now that Jade is in kindergarten and the boys are enrolled in day care, these late nights rarely occur.

A new relationship is woven over time. The one unique thing Brian gives them—that the kids share with him—is his stories. He has the capacity to have them sitting on their chairs after the pizza has been demolished. These are the stories from the only time in life that kids find remotely interesting—childhood.

"Uncle Brian, tell us about when Johnny got bit by the monkey."

"Yeah, yeah, tell that one."

Brian takes a deep, thoughtful breath as they lean forward to take it all in. "Well," he starts, "once my brother . . ." And continues to describe his memory of the time his youngest brother was bitten by a monkey on the way home from school.

"No, Uncle Brian," Darren corrects. "He said 'Mommy, Mommy, I got bit by a monkey.' "

"I'm coming to that, Darren."

Deven jumps the gun. "And then your mommy said he wasn't."

The kids and Brian basically compete to finish the story.

Brian hasn't finished the last word of this particular story when Jade jumps in. "Uncle Brian, tell how that time you were a little boy and you were at the beach and you won the fish."

Darren can't help himself. "And it went down your mommy's shirt."

They start giggling at the prospect of the story, especially because the goldfish he won ended up flipping between his mother's "boobies." Darren always laughs so hard he lets himself fall off the chair.

After the real-life adventures come Brian's own brand of story that he cultivated many years ago when we first started dating and my sister Rachel was just three. It's the Cooper Carney series. Cooper has all kinds of relatives—like Blarney Carney from Ireland and Chili con Carney from Mexico. On and on.

As the kids get older, they start telling their own silly anecdotes that they always laugh their way through, making them impossible to understand. It is difficult for anyone to "get it," but the point of storytelling with friends around a table, whether you understand the words or not, is joy.

SICK AT SCHOOL

*D*even got sick at preschool. Raina picks him up early from the youngest threes group. It's not all that unusual for him to pick up bugs and go from feeling okay to shooting up to 102°. But now he's limping and complaining of pain in his right leg. Raina decides not to let it wait till the morning. She calls the doctor's office after hours and they tell her to bring him in. Raina's mom, Elizabeth, still lives with them, but isn't home from a church function yet, so Raina asks me to come over and stay with Jade and Darren till Elizabeth gets in. It's 10:30 P.M. I'm in my bathrobe. "I'll be there in ten minutes."

"Good," she says. "I may need some help getting him in the car."

When I get there, Deven, who is usually really cranky when he's sick, is absolutely still. When he gets up to walk, Raina notices that the limp is even worse than when she picked him up at school. They make it to the car with no problem.

Elizabeth returns an hour later. We discuss the limp, and Elizabeth is certain that it wasn't there yesterday, so he must have just hurt his leg playing.

OUT OF LEFT FIELD

*R*aina calls the next afternoon. I give her a breezy hello, totally forgetting Deven's doctor's visit the night before.

She cuts me off. "Martha . . . I have some bad news. Deven has leukemia."

"But how could he go from being fine to having leukemia?" I protest.

"I don't know. They have to do more tests to find out what kind and how bad. He just got admitted to the hospital."

"What can we do?" I ask.

"Well, I'm staying over tonight with him. He's getting anesthesia now for some procedure. . . . I don't know. . . . Maybe one of you can come sit with him for a few hours so I can go see the other kids. You know, I just left last night like I was running out for a doctor's appointment. They don't know what's going on."

"You know we'll come whenever . . . just call," I tell her. She gives me the phone number for his room, but I tell her I won't bother her there. She can call when she wants. "Oh, Raina," I manage to get out before crying.

"Martha," she says, knowing what she's asking from me. "Pray for him . . . and all of us."

"I promise . . . but is there anything more I can *do*?"

I'm wanting something "better" than prayer.

"Not right now," she says softly. "Just pray."

WORSE NEWS

$\mathcal{R}$aina calls later. "Deven doesn't have leukemia," she announces.

"Oh, thank God!"

"It's worse: he has neuroblastoma."

Oh no. I don't know much, but I know that neuroblastoma is a lot worse than leukemia for most kids. It is a cancer of early childhood. The majority of children have it detected before the age of five. At three, Deven fits right in. The most common symptoms come from a tumor mass or from bone pain, because by the time it comes to the attention of health care professionals, the cancer has usually metastasized. Children of any age with localized neuroblastoma—meaning a tumor limited to one place—have the highest rate of survival. Infants under the age of one have a more optimistic prognosis.

Other children whose cancers have spread from the original sites have tougher times. One study I read used very aggressive chemotherapy that resulted in a two-year survival rate of only 20 percent of the more seriously ill children. Unfortunately, further testing shows that Deven is Stage 4, which means that the disease has disseminated to distant lymph nodes, bone marrow, and the liver.

While the exact course of treatment hasn't been formulated, it's clear to me from a very discouraging journey on the Internet that Deven is looking at surgery for the original tumor, aggressive and possibly experimental chemotherapy, radiation, and bone marrow transplants. Originally, I'd planned to put together the information for Raina. But information overload is *my* way of coping, and this time it's not even helping *me*. With horrible news there is sometimes solace in dosing the bad news to the smallest of swallows. Otherwise you'll choke. But just the word "neuroblastoma"; I can't get beyond that without feeling like I'm going to implode.

THE LONG HAUL BEGINS

*R*aina calls from the hospital, where she's been since Deven was admitted.

"I need a break. He won't let go of me," she says wearily.

I'm fifteen minutes from the hospital and tell her I'll throw some clothes on and be right over. Then I realize that going to that hospital means driving on Route 50, not knowing the right cutoff, and being really, really nervous. But, I reassure myself, it's Sunday, traffic won't be bad.

I miss the exit, inciting my greatest fear: being totally lost. From a psychological perspective it is probably some kind of metaphor, but I don't care, because at the moment I am definitely geographically displaced. The lack of typical traffic allows me to screw up several times with little consequence. By the time I reach the hospital, I realize that my hands hurt because they've been clenched so tightly around the steering wheel. My back is sore because I've been hunched over, trying to figure out where I'm going, like those old ladies I always curse on the road.

I already start to worry about driving home, hoping the traffic doesn't pick up much, wondering when the Redskins game is scheduled, figuring that traffic will decrease during the broadcast. I despise this part of myself, worrying about such stupid things while my friend is not far away, dealing with every parent's ultimate nightmare.

Raina wants to see Jade and Darren and collect things to bring back. What she is facing is so devastating, I don't know how she can breathe. When she starts to say good-bye, Deven acts like he will never see her again. Just transferring him from her to me takes fifteen minutes. His legs and arms are locked around her.

"Don't leave me. Mommy, don't leave me. Mommy, take me home," he screams and pleads. It is killing her.

Finally I mouth the words, "Just go. It will be okay." She pries his arms from her, and the anguish in his voice makes me feel like there's a part of me caving in.

I hold him while he cries and try to interest him in the gift I brought. He continues to cry, his arms tightly encircling my neck. I can feel the tension in his little legs as he wraps them around my hips to keep us connected. I trip over the IV pole. He has already started chemotherapy and is wired to a beeping machine. At one point, we become so entangled in all the tubes and the IV pole that I have to ring for a nurse to undo us. She helps me sit in the lounge chair with him still wrapped around me, shows me the VCR and the videos, and tells us that Ronald McDonald is coming for a visit. Deven allows me to carry him to see Ronald and then is so totally unimpressed with the cheap plastic goodies being given out that he makes the assessment, "No nuggets, who cares?" And we return to his room.

He finally settles down to play with the present I brought him, a video of *Blue's Clues*, his current candidate for coolest thing on TV. Blue is a big dog, who along with his friend Steve—a real guy, who always wears the same green-on-green striped shirt—solves riddles with clues and a trusty notebook. We watch the video and he uses Blue's Handy Dandy notebook and crayon I got for him to play along. He calms down, although any move I make signals possible abandonment, and he requires constant reassurance and makes the demand that I sit still.

An hour later I realize I should have gone to the bathroom before Raina left. Even though each room has its own bathroom, there's no way I'm leaving him now. After another twenty minutes, it is clear that there is no choice, *I have to go.* I tell Deven that I just have to sit him down in the chair himself for a minute so that I can go. No way! So we have to get ourselves unhooked from the wall, and, trailing the unwieldy IV pole, Deven and I go to the bathroom together.

He won't even let me put him on the floor so I can sit down. It is like some disaster will happen if his feet touch the floor. If it wasn't so awful—trying to pee with a boy sitting on your lap, who is hooked up to a pole, with a bunch of flashing lights and tubes and beeping sounds that I pray to God we don't get all mixed up again—it would be sort of funny. I really don't want to have to call the nurse with a small boy on my lap and my underpants around my knees.

It doesn't matter. One machine, wired directly into the nurses' station, beckons a nurse. I hear her calling and marching in. I'm not finished and I've left the door ajar. Deven tells me to hurry up, but pulling your pants up when you have a kid on you isn't easy. The nurse catches me in the act. I can see by the look on her face that she's wondering *Who the hell are you?*

She reaches for Deven, who instantly recoils and starts screaming, "Aunt Martha!"

What followed would become a constant refrain in all tones, volumes, tenors, and moods: "Lemme 'lone!!!"

She starts to lecture him loudly about how he's going to have to learn to let grown-ups have some time off. I still haven't gotten my pants all the way up. He is wrapped around me and kicks the nurse every time she gets close. There's a part of me thinking *Go ahead. Nail her.*

She insists on checking the machine, which somehow we managed to maneuver into the small bathroom. Now all three of us are wedged in. I'd really like to flush. He'd really like to kill the nurse. She keeps lecturing him in this singsong voice that some adults, who think they know how to talk to children, but are actually incredibly out of touch, use—always to no avail. She adjusts the machine, and I reassure her that we can get back across the room unassisted (which, in all honesty, is not a bet I'd take).

For the next several hours I crave anything to drink—even the crappy apple juice they serve at room temperature in those little plastic cups. But the thought of reliving the bathroom fiasco is enough to keep me parched.

Raina walks through the door, and no child has ever been

so happy to see his mother. "You came!!" he yells, like there was ever a question.

As I try to fill her in on who came by, who called, and what they said, Deven interjects loudly: "I peed with Aunt Martha!"

I feel my face go from pale to sunburnt in a matter of seconds.

Raina listens as we take turns describing it. I tell her I'll put money on the fact that she'll get some sly inquiries about "that Aunt Martha person" who was with Deven.

Once his mother arrives, Deven can barely acknowledge my existence and has no intention of even saying good-bye to me. I walk to the car, laughing to myself about the bathroom incident.

But then I remember where it happened and why it happened and how in the course of twenty-four hours Deven has gone from day care—overflowing with high-octane kids—to the Pediatric Oncology Unit where weakened, bald, crying children are now his neighbors. A horrible illness has picked him up like a tornado, and it could even take him away, erase his existence in a world that is just getting used to him.

Now I can't find my parking ticket. Then I can't find my car. I lean against a garbage can and cry. And I watch my every exhalation as it diffuses into the crisp autumn afternoon. Someone slams the door of a car nearby, and I tell myself to straighten up, but I just keep on crying. I don't care who sees me. Hell, no way this is the first breakdown in that garage.

CHEMO, STEM CELL TRANSPLANTS, AND PUBLIC RELATIONS

The pediatric oncologists get to work quickly with a plan to surgically remove the original tumor, then begin aggres-

sive chemotherapy. On the basis of his response, the next step
is an autologous stem cell transplant (where Deven's own cells
are cleaned up with chemotherapy and then harvested). It would
be far better if there was a match from someone else. Darren
would have been the best shot, of course. If they were identical
twins, it would be a far better shot. But the bad news reaches
us that no one in his family is a match. It's a long, tough
process. They do two stem cell transplants.

Deven is an absolute pain to the hospital staff. Raina and
I joke that we think most of them flip a coin on the shift and
the loser gets him. I don't blame them on one level—he raises
holy hell at any intrusion, even something as innocuous as a
thermometer or blood pressure cuff. It pains Raina to see him
falling apart, regressing to that little volcano he was at two,
and doing it so publicly. She is afraid of the implication that
she is a bad mother. Everyone who knows him tries to make it
clear that Deven has always been on the tightly wound side,
but with this stress, it's extreme even for him.

Over the course of months, one thing that helps is for his
mom or an auntie or me—or someone else he knows well—to
perform the basic procedures that have to be done: place him
on the scale, which he despises; put the blood pressure cuff on;
the thermometer in his ear; the stethoscope in the right place.
The worst is feeding him oral medicine, which is a regular, sometimes bloody—in terms of bites and scratches—battleground.
It's like he's fighting for his life against the very people who are
trying to help save it.

In the big picture, he weathers all the major stuff like a
trouper. The surgeries and the chemo actually go fairly well.
Even when he vomits continually, he does so matter-of-factly,
trying to return to his video or book as quickly as possible. I
believe his feistiness is something to be admired on some level;

it's getting him through this. The trick is finding ways of cooling things down with the staff. It's a long process, full of meetings, where at some point I am referred to as Raina's psychologist, which she stiffly corrects.

"She's my girlfriend," she usually says or "She's Deven's aunt." But I can still tell that everyone wonders who the hell I am and how I fit in the picture. It's easy early on to dismiss me as working in some kind of official role. It gets harder when they see me there all day, in bed with Deven, having the range of loving affection and stern limit-setting that is more appropriate to friends and family than professional helper.

This is confirmed most stridently by the little man himself when a nurse starts introducing him and then me to a technician of some sort. She says in the slow, happy, loud way adults sometimes talk to each other in front of kids, "This is Deven and his social worker—I'm sorry, what's your name?"

Deven looks at her like she's claiming she's spotted an asteroid. He sits straight up and points to me. "She's not a *worker, she's my aunt Martha!*"

"Yep, that's who I am," I confirm.

They look totally confused, which for some reason I like. I don't spend much time in this friendship twisting and turning about race. But when we are in public, I can't help it. More than our presence together, it's the *ways* Brian, Raina, and I relate to one another and our kids that leave people scratching their heads. If Brian and I were black, no one at the hospital would give us a second look. We'd be friends or family and that would be that. But on the basis of my color, and probably to some extent the age difference between Raina and me, I am something to be "figured out." It feels strange.

ANOTHER ROUND

*D*even is in for his stem cell transplant. He lies there, all of his twenty-nine pounds, with eight drugs—benign poisons—dripping into his veins. He has scars, catheters, "tubies" coming from the central line that was surgically implanted at the beginning of his treatment. It prevents his constantly being stuck with needles. He has gotten so used to it all that he casually calls, "I'm beeping," when one machine or another signals that it needs a nurse's attention.

Deven has fought hard against the whole process—having some inner wisdom that has him leaving the absolutely critical things in place and singularly waging war on the more trivial stuff. The central line stays in place, but the thermometers and the spoonfuls of medicine take flight as he fights them with everything he's got.

I LOVE YOU, YOU LOVE ME

*T*he first song we sang with the two-year-old boys was "I love you, you love me," the theme song of *Barney*, which was originally cute and got old real fast. But during these long days in the hospital I don't know what we'd do without Barney and his videos. It is a surer shot than a sedative to calm Deven down. Even as he continues hiccuping and wiping his runny nose or eyes, he burrows in and focuses on the video as if complete attention is integral to his survival. And perhaps, at these moments, it is. He has memorized the entire video: the trailers, the very last note at the end of the very last song where the

credits giving acknowledgment to the guy who brought bagels
to the set every day are rolling. He knows every word, every
inflection. He's got the rhythms and tones of every speaking
voice. His still fragile voice wraps itself around Barney's, and
he sets off reciting the full tape like a long prayer, a sappy purple mantra.

He is perfectly attuned to me, especially as he senses my attention lapsing. At these moments he is always glued to me in
the hospital room recliner or stretched out with his head on my
chest in his bed. "What comes next?" he'll demand. A pop quiz
out of nowhere, attempting to assess the progress of my
memory since our viewing of the tape two hours ago. His has
little patience for my errors. He loves to take me to task in one
breath and forgive me the next.

"You don't remember. You didn't pay attention. . . ." he
scolds. But then he always takes my face in his little hands, be-
stows a loving glance, and says, "But it's okay. You didn't mean
it. You'll do better next time."

"Do you think so?" I ask with concern, dreading the next
time we have to endure this video, even with the opportunities
for redemption. He accommodates his little body to me, even
though it is tethered to a pole that beeps continually and pumps
his system with poisons that hopefully will wage war on the
diseased cells that stand in the way of a healthy Deven.

Barney winds down. Shadows fall across the windows. Another helicopter hovers near Shock Trauma. In the early days
of Deven's hospitalizations, these landings were the best show
in town. Now they're only background noise. While the nurses
and doctors register the numbers on Deven's many machines, I
am more aware of the clock. It's been five hours. I thought
Raina would be here by now. It's time for me to go. I need to
stretch, get a soda, roll over in the bed. It's like he reads my
mind, like Deven knows I'm looking to bolt. He grabs my arm

before I can make a move and says the dreaded word, "Again." He wants to watch *Barney* again. He wants to remain encircled in my body where he lies against my chest. He wants to forget his growing anxiety that there may be a gap between my leaving and his mother's coming—something that will not happen.

"Okay, okay," I bargain. "Don't you want to eat some of this dinner at least while we rewind?"

He wisely refuses. I remain amazed at how far afield hospital nutritionists and cooks have to go to produce the unappetizing food they do. They are one step away from the elementary school lunches I sampled on visits to my daughter's school. I'm not a food snob: I basically draw the line at beef jerky and those hard-boiled eggs in jars on store counters. If a restaurant has a drive-through, I won't turn my nose up at much on the menu. I thought I had no standards. I thought I had never liked hospital food because I was too sick to eat. Now I know the essential reason: it is uniformly and supremely disgusting. When I try to coax Deven to take a bite out of something resembling a Chicken McNugget, no dice. He wants his favorite "pannycakes" from McDonald's, which, of course aren't available on Sunday evenings.

I sense a tantrum and head it off with a preemptive bribe. "How about a trip to the candy machine?" We need to get permission from a nurse and have to swear we'll be no more than five minutes before she agrees to unhook him enough so he can push the multilayered, beeping machine of medicines while he walks. His two feet hit the floor and it's like he's just touched an electrified grid.

He jumps into my arms, settles himself on my hip, and we both push the pole. He is determined to "do the money" and choose the candy—tough because it involves pushing a number code to select the candy. We practice pressing 2 and then 3 several times before putting the money in. It works. He is more pleased with himself than he is with the candy. There are so few chances in his situation to exert his will and his ability on something and make it happen. I tell him how proud I am of him, and he returns the compliment. "You were good, too."

As I carry him back to the room, he notices the scratch on my cheek. He touches it gently and asks if it hurts. "Where'd you get it?"

"You scratched me on the face."

"No I didn't," he insists, looking a bit horrified.

"Yeah, you did. Remember this morning when you were so mad about the medicine and how I had to help the nurse give it to you?"

"Oh." There's a moment of quiet. "Are you mad at me?" he asks softly.

"When you did it, I felt mad because it hurt. And I don't wanna keep getting scratched."

He traces the cut on my cheek. "Do you still love me?"

"Deven, remember what we talked about—you, Darren, Jade, and me? That there is nothing you can do to make me not love you?"

"Yeah, even when we breaked stuff."

"And stuff even worse than that. There is *nothing* you can do to make me stop loving you."

"Yeah."

"But, Deven, we still have to figure out another way for you to let people know how unhappy you are."

"Yeah . . . but, Aunt Martha?"

"Yes, honey?"

"Will you open this candy for me?"

TAKE NO PRISONERS

I get off the elevator at Pediatrics. As I round the corner to pass the protective automatic door labeled Pediatric Oncology, I can already hear Deven. His mom told me his room was being changed, so I thought I was going to have to ask at the nurses' desk. But I don't need to—I can follow the screaming. He is surrounded by three nurses.

Deven believes that the best defense is a strong preemptive offense. And over time he has moved from a sweet, cuddly boy to one who maximizes elbows, fingernails, feet, toenails, and teeth. He takes no prisoners, knocking off glasses, scratching faces, trying to take a chomp out of any hand that dares come close. He twists and bucks, all twenty-nine pounds of him. To enter the room and see nurses restraining this poor, wailing creature, it is easy to imagine what horrible things they are trying to do to him: spinal tap, new IV, skin biopsy. No. Deven is a champ with the big stuff. Unbelievably strong and pain tolerant.

Today, he is marshaling everything in him to resist a simple thermometer in his ear or under his arm. A routine, every hour, no more than a two-minute procedure. If it's not the thermometer, he's balking at the stethoscope that has already been thoughtfully prewarmed for his chest. He refuses his oral medications. For the staff he is a major problem.

Sometimes I encircle him, holding his arms in a half hug half restraint, talking in his ear, voicing feelings he may be having while rocking him gently. When that doesn't work, four nurses hold an arm or a leg, someone holds his head back, and I squeeze his cheeks while a nurse literally forces him to take his medicine. We keep his head back until he has to swallow. If he outsmarts us, we all end up smelling like bubble gum and the whole thing has to be repeated. He is enraged as he looks up at the heads and hands bent over him. His single goal in life becomes spitting out as much medicine as he can.

Sometimes, on the long afternoons when I'm subbing for Raina, I find myself getting angrier and angrier at him. I'm mad because he won't do what will make him better, and I can't stand being scratched and bitten. When I've had just about enough—and the nurses, who still can't figure out who I am, but expect me to have the magic to coach him through—I raise my voice above his screaming. "Stop it, Deven, just stop it! Stop it right now!" It's like an injection where I'm only doing it for his own good. But it usually works.

When I startle him with my very firm and angry voice, his anger shifts to grief, from charged to exhausted, from warrior to prisoner of war. The screams turn to wails, then sobs. The contorted face lets go. Tears that were locked away are now streaming down his cheeks. His body relaxes, and all he wants is to be held and shushed and rocked. He sniffles and hiccups and echoes the same laments: "I don't want it. I want my mommy. I want to go home."

Soon he is limp, exhausted, and somewhat more open to compromise. "What if you put the thermometer under your arm yourself?" Or "What about you decide which medicine you're going to take *first*." Then the ultimate bribe, the one that is pure joy for him and for me, pure punishment. "Hurry up. Because as soon as you finish, we can watch . . . Barney!" He takes his medicine. I turn on the video. It's time to take mine.

HOME

I wanna go home!" Deven wails his lament as a mantra again and again, but each refrain has no greater effect than his first. Home? What is home to Deven? All the stuff that comes with three children has overwhelmed his apartment. It is so crowded it's impossible to keep everything in its place. Nothing really had a place to start with. The blinds are usually pulled for privacy, leaving the place begging for light, only partially redeemed by a lamp or two. Space is absent—covered or claimed.

His hospital room is private and bright. He has a built-in TV and VCR with a full library of videos and no one to fight with about them. People visit and bring him gifts. He presses a button and gets what he wants. Because he is so remarkably resilient, he often doesn't feel too terrible from the treatments. But he wants to go home, no matter where that is. He wants the feeling of belonging to a place and the people who share it with him. At his most upset, when he cries for home, he cries for Mom.

Home is mother, and for a long time she's the closest you can get to reenacting the womb. That first home is soil so conducive to growth. It's the atmosphere, the garden, the seedling, and water all rolled into one. It is the sweet, shadowy, fluid domain in which a mother buffers her child from a world he's not ready to meet. It is everything. From birth on imports and exports will become a continual theme. "How do I get that feeling? How do I keep it?" We bring things, make things, or repair or buy things to enhance that sense of home.

When we think of the word "home," what comes to mind? The home we live in now? The place we were raised? Or does this place reside in a person, someone whose very presence envelopes us and allows us finally to let go? And rest.

THE POSSIBILITIES

I'm in the midst of an overworked sentence for an overdue magazine article.

The number of Raina's office pops up on caller ID. She's been working as a secretary, but the amount she's spending for child care is almost negating the money she makes on the job. But she wants to be self-sufficient and be a good example to her kids. The whole thing overwhelms her.

I have *got* to get this thing done and I know we'll end up chatting forever, but I pick up anyway. "Hello," I say, trying to sound like I'm in the middle of real business.

"Hey, it's me."

"Hey, you," I respond, glad that I can tell from her tone that nothing is wrong.

"My boss just left for a while. She is such a pain. Everything is by the clock. And she doesn't just come out and say she's not happy about something, she has these looks like she's suckin' on lemons. I wish she'd just come out and say it. Nobody likes her."

"That's why I'm so glad I work for myself. . . . Of course, that leaves *me* having to call myself an asshole—Whoops! Sorry for the language."

"You're a mess." She chuckles.

"So what else is new?"

"Oh, I know what I wanted to tell you," she tells me. "You know my girlfriend Tamara—remember her baby's father

walked out on her and then she found out she was pregnant
again? You know—she's real funny. . . . Anyway, she's been
going through a rough time."

"I think so. . . ."

"Well, she got qualified to get a house through this program where you don't pay very much to buy it, but you and
your family and friends and then other volunteers and experts
fix up old houses or build new ones and it's yours. You own it.
The money you pay every month isn't rent. It's all yours."

"I've heard of that program," I break in. "It's Habitat for
Humanity. It's amazing."

"Yeah, Habitat. That's what it is. She just found out she's
qualified, and you know all those row houses near Old Town—
people are fixing them up and they're worth a lot. Habitat has
taken a few houses and they are going to totally fix them inside
and out. Inside, they will look like brand-new houses—new appliances, everything. And outside they'll make them match the
neighborhood and put in trees and bushes and stuff. Can you
believe it? And listen to this," she continues. "The down payment is incredibly low."

"Are you kidding me?"

"No, but first she has to put in all these hours working on
her house and the other peoples' houses. It's hard. But then she
pays every month and, guess what—it's a lot less than her rent.
And it's *her home*."

"God, I wish they had more," I wish aloud.

"That's the best part!" Raina exclaims. "They give each
person a partner to work with, sort of like a bridge to the Habitat organization. Anyway, her partner told her that Habitat has
plans to build new houses in Arlington. I don't know how many
or where, but, Martha, could you believe it? Getting my own
house? The basic design on all the houses is the same, but I can

make decisions about colors and tiles and carpeting. Now you really have to save all those catalogues you put aside for me."

"How do you find out about it?"

"She's gonna call her partner and get a name or a number."

"Oh, Raina, I promise I'll start saying my prayers right now."

"I know it's crazy, with everything going on with Deven that I even *think* about doing something like this. . . ."

"I don't know, but in some ways it makes a lot of sense. Things are so over the top, that just for it to come up as a possibility . . . It's all about future . . . and hope . . . y'know?" We're both quiet for a few seconds.

"I'm gonna get the number. But, you know, I'm worried about filling in the application. I always get nervous when I have to fill out—like, you know, I told you before—like essay questions . . . and then I put it off till it's too late."

"Never fear, my friend. I may not be able to slam a nail straight into a wall, but honey, I am the *queen of bullshit*." She starts laughing. "I'm not kidding. All of Keara's friends—except Keara, herself, who would rather eat dirt than ask me for help—and then for several years their younger brothers and sisters came over, and I helped them with their college applications. I didn't write them. It wasn't cheating. It was just helping them find their own voices and then following the questions logically. And basically helping them not to undersell themselves. Same thing with this."

"Martha, wouldn't it be a blessing?" She says it like she's a kid standing at the entrance to Disney World.

"Oh, Raina, *it's got to be.*"

HABITAT FOR HUMANITY

J first heard about Habitat through former president Jimmy Carter and his wife, Rosalynn, on TV. They were getting down and dirty in T-shirts and jeans, leather belts, and tools, working up real sweat. But that's about all I knew. In my hunger for helpful information, I searched the Web. The organization, which is like no other, was founded in 1976 by Millard and Linda Fuller, a financially comfortable couple who abandoned that life for a totally different pursuit. They started a nonprofit, ecumenical, Christian housing ministry (although it is respectful of all religions and not evangelical). They decided that housing was one of the most basic of all needs, and the housing situation in this country and others, is dire.

Home ownership in very-low-income families with children has actually fallen. Government housing subsidies are the least likely to assist the very poor with children. According to a HUD report, 5.4 million households containing 12.3 million people face the worst-case housing needs. These are renters who receive no government assistance, who make less than 50 percent of the median income, and pay either more than 50 percent of their income for rent and utilities or live in housing with severe physical deficiencies. Particularly disturbing is the nearly ten million households with kids who live in the midst of significant lead paint poisons. The rates of asthma among poor urban children are skyrocketing, creating a culture of kids walking around with inhalers, at risk of lifelong respiratory disease.

Fuller says, "The opposite of grace is disgrace. Our choice is between grace and disgrace. Do we want graceful communities where love and concern abound, or disgraceful ones, where love and concern are withheld and dispersed to only a privileged few?" What I personally love about this mandate is that it is not just rich people being nice and helping poor people, it's reciprocal. He emphasizes that "what the poor need is not charity but capital, not caseworkers but coworkers. And what the rich need is a wise, honorable, and just way of divesting themselves of their overabundance."

Habitat is an ingenious blend of corporate, community, and faith-based organizations combined with volunteers and future homeowners. So far, 125,000 homes have been refurbished or built, housing 625,000 people.

The homes are sold to families at no profit, with low down payments and low-interest loans. The home owner must become a partner with Habitat before she ever plunks down any cash or moves in the furniture. In lieu of a large down payment, the partner must put in sweat equity—hours of working alongside volunteers, as well as expert carpenters, electricians, roofers, and plumbers—to build other houses and then assist with her own.

To be considered for the program, Raina will have to fill in a rather lengthy form that scared her, providing information about income, expenses, special needs, and so forth. If accepted, she will have to attend classes on all aspects of home ownership—from taxes to small household repairs and troubleshooting. Before qualifying as a partner, she'll have to put in fifty hours of sweat equity, which would then be applied to her total required hours if she is accepted. Then she would be able to assign some of her hours to willing family and friends. Fortunately, the down payment is not due until she officially takes ownership of the finished house.

Right now I'm especially interested in the eight units breaking ground at the corner of Kenmore and Glebe roads, about one mile from here. The timing stinks. It's so much work. But, hell, even I can handle a hammer.

SOMEONE NEW

*R*aina has met someone. She's been working part-time at Harris Teeter, a new grocery store in the neighborhood. Every now and then she mentioned a guy named William. At first they hung out together during breaks. Then they went out for quick dinners after work. She always played it down, emphasizing that they were just friends.

But now it's official. They're more than friends. She seems to really like him. He's a nice guy. A bit older than Raina. Soft-spoken and gentle with the kids. Raina's taken him to church, and he's been great with Deven—enduring hospital nights and long doctors' office days. I'm terrible about things like this. Whether it's Keara or Raina, with any new guy I'm always thinking, *husband material*? I have to work to keep my mouth shut. But I like him. Brian likes him. Who knows? Maybe he's a keeper.

THE VINEYARD

*B*rian and I accompany Raina to the first meeting for families who might be interested in becoming one of the eight partners in the ownership of town houses Habitat will build in Arlington. There are over one hundred people at the meeting—a combination of families, friends, community, and Habitat higher-ups. They open with a lovely prayer. Brian and Raina have their eyes closed in silent reflection, but I can't help myself. I use the time to scope out the competition. There are way too many people here, and I am in gear about how Raina is going to prevail over all these other people.

There's a family in front of us: five little boys, a white father, and a Vietnamese mother. The boys run wild, loud and out of control. I fume about these people. If they can't keep their children in check, well then, they shouldn't qualify. The prayer is over and now some official is talking about Habitat, so I continue to look around. I am aware of my complete and total pettiness, but I can't help myself. I want this for her so much. She deserves it. More than these other people I know nothing about.

Raina is always thrilled when I prove that I'm not a total heathen, but the truth is that there are many passages of Scripture that have great import for me. Sometimes they are of comfort. More often, they are like the mosquito bite on the very place on my back that I can't reach. They irritate me because I have to struggle to understand them. Understanding often involves a push for painful self-knowledge or change.

There was a vineyard owner who needed to hire workers to assist him in his harvest. It wasn't clear how much help he needed, so he started out first thing in the morning and hired men with an agreement of a set wage for the day's work. Later, when it became clear that he needed more help, he got more workers, gave them the same promise for the day's wage. Toward the end of the afternoon, he saw that he still needed help, so he hired some latecomers with the same understanding of the day's wage. At the end of the day, when they all lined up to be paid, the guys who had come early in the morning were infuriated that their pay was the same as the latecomers'. The guys from the early afternoon then registered their unhappiness. And the latecomers gladly took their cash. Everyone but the latecomers was furious with the vineyard owner, who basically said, "Didn't I give you exactly what we agreed upon?" The answer was yes.

Always for me a "yes . . . but!!!!" That's the Martha Manning story. I have a burning desire to find some way of making things fairer.

That's what I feel like now: It's not fair.

In the crowd I see a couple of people we know through neighborhood associations and old PTA work. I keep elbowing Brian and saying, "What's that guy's name?" And once he's searched his unbelievable memory and given me an answer, I suggest, "Maybe afterward you can introduce him to Raina." No response. I do that a couple of times until he basically tells me to shut up. Raina is paying attention, following some forms they're going through, and I'm working up to an anxiety attack that we won't do everything we possibly can to get Raina what she deserves.

I don't like this part of myself. At all.

THE OTHER KIDS

*D*arren and Jade are having their own trials. Jade, who has just turned six, is feeling ignored and is angry, with few outlets for expression of her needs or her anger. Raina tries to give her alone time, but practical considerations make that hard.

At four, Darren is quickly becoming the "bad boy." There is no doubt—he is loud and energetic. He is relentless with "why" questions. It's usually best just to say "I don't know" right away, because every answer you offer will open the door to another question. In the old days he'd have been called "all boy." Cloistered in that tiny apartment with several extra people and a grandmother who is far less approving of him than his mother just compounds his anguish for missing things the way they used to be. He gets into fights at preschool. He wets his pants. He is angry and sad. He adores the mother who has been taken from him so precipitously. The loss of his lifelong partner in crime, Deven, is of great confusion to him.

Neither he nor Jade understand Deven's illness. Most of the time when they visit the hospital, Deven is just cranky and selfish, not wanting to share any of the considerable stash of gifts he's amassed. They often have to spend long hours in that hot room, watching video after video, making just enough noise and commotion to warrant dirty looks from some of the staff. When Raina goes to the kitchen to microwave some soup or fix them some cereal that is always kept on hand, she's told by some snippy nurse that the food is for patients only and given directions to the cafeteria. The only thing worse than the food in the cafeteria is the prices.

Deven refuses to eat his food, and when Raina lets the other kids have it, she gets reprimanded again. When she finally catches her breath she stocks up on those Styrofoam noodle packs and other things that she can just add water and microwave for Jade and Darren. But as convenient and cheap as those noodle packs are, I can say from experience that they get real old real fast.

MIRACLES OF MEDICINE

*D*even's treatment is working. After two transplants, megachemotherapy, surgeries, and, to top it off, a huge hit of radiation, he is clean. No neuroblastoma. Anywhere. His little bald head starts to fill out with straight, downy black hair. He's grown an inch. His weight is the same, but his appetite is great. His color is back and he's calmed down. He wants to get back to regular life. He won't be allowed to be close to other children for at least six months to a year. If Darren or Jade get sick, Deven has to be isolated. If his fever goes above 100, he has to go back to the hospital. Otherwise, "normal life" will be constant trips to the oncologists' office for labs, transfusions, platelets, and follow-up testing.

In some ways, this is tougher on Raina day to day, because she can now spend full days at the doctors' office waiting for procedures, dealing with Deven's distress and anger that he still has to undergo the things he hates only he doesn't stay over at the hospital. He reprises his awful behavior acclimation process for getting used to the different staff at the doctors' office. The child care that was funded by the county when Raina had a job has been withdrawn since she had to leave her job as a cashier at Harris Teeter. She tried to work nights, so she could cover the doctors' visits and Deven's care. But she couldn't stretch the coverage of the kids, with friends and relatives.

Now, most days, Darren has to accompany them. It makes for a very long day. But Deven is in remission.

"Remission" is a beautiful word.

THE APPLICATION

*I*t's midday and I'm under deadline for a magazine piece. It's not going well, and then, of course, the phone rings. I hate the phone. And my attention is so easily derailed by the original ring that whatever thought I'd been entertaining is long gone by time the actual message comes through.

Every time I sit down at my desk, the first thing I do is turn off the volume of the machine, so I am not distracted by human voices. But sitting there struggling with the empty silence of writer's block I hear the click, click, click. A blinking light comes on the smaller caller-ID machine, and although I've purposely placed it outside my peripheral vision, I want to know who is calling, even though I don't want to talk to him.

Raina's number comes up on the machine. I turn up the volume on the answering machine.

"Martha, I know you're writing. Don't pick up. I'm just leaving a message. Just want to tell you that I am holding the Habitat for Humanity application form. You should see it. . . ."

I'm groping around for my glasses so I can find the right button on the right machine that will let me talk to her directly.

Bingo. I hit the right button. "Raina, Raina, stop. I've got it."

"Martha, is that you? Yeah. I mean it's only the application. You won't believe it. It's scary. I'm not kidding. It would be easier to build the house than fill this whole thing in. They're gonna have eight town houses. Two and three bedrooms. Front and backyards. They're gonna be really nice. Let's see it—it's seven, no, nine pages! Oh no! It says some of the questions should be completed on a separate piece of paper. You know how long those ones are!" Her enthusiasm begins to deflate as she continues describing the form.

"Raina, don't worry about it at all. When's it due?"

"Two weeks."

"Okay, how about if you come by so I can see it and get an idea of what they're looking for?"

"Well, some of it is easy—names and ages of the kids, how much money I have coming in—but then they ask you stuff like, 'Why do you want to become a Habitat family?' I mean, how am I supposed to answer stuff like that?"

"Listen, Raina, like I told you, I am really good at this. It's the fine art of bullshit."

She laughs, but reminds me, "I have to tell the truth."

"I'm not talking about lying, and I'm not talking about *me* doing it instead of *you*. There's just a way of breaking down a question into parts, getting clear on everything you need to get in there, and then—let's call it 'finessing it.' You know like gift wrapping a toaster."

"Gift wrapping a toaster?" She laughs. "Have you stopped sleeping again?"

"No, it's like you're taking this practical, necessary, basic but possibly a little bit boring thing . . . so you get pretty paper and ribbon and dress it up a little."

"Makes sense," she concedes. "Can you still make copies off your broken fax machine?"

"Hold on, let me check." I put a piece of paper through and it works. "Yeah, it works. Not well, but it's okay, Why?"

"I was thinking I'd drop by later, make a copy to leave with you, and we could set a time to get together to work on it when I don't have the kids."

"Brian's working late. I'm here all night."

"How's it going?" she asks.

"Lousy . . . I'm boring myself."

"Cheer up. See you later."

"See ya."

At 8:00 I'm sitting down to watch some worthless show on TV. After a knock on the door, the kids, puffy in their snowsuits, fall through the door, with energy I can only get with at least four major hits of caffeine. Deven brings up the rear with an A for effort. Raina follows, toting her bags and theirs. It looks like they're planning to spend the night. *Oh God, I thought this was going to be a five-minute copy job.*

"Aunt Martha, do you have anything to eat?" Jade asks.

"Didn't you have dinner?" I reply.

"No."

"Yes, you did," Raina interrupts, annoyed. "You just didn't *eat* it."

"I hate macaroni and cheese," she whines.

"You can have a PBJ," I offer.

"No," in three voices.

"Grilled cheese sandwich."

"No!"

"Cinnamon toast—*my final offer.*"

"With hot cocoa?" asks Darren.

"Yes."

"With marshmallows?" Deven asks.

"No marshmallows."

"Awww."

"Oh, will you all cut me a break. I'm out of marshmallows!"

"You didn't used to be," accuses Deven.

"I used them up when I was baking something."

"*What* were you baking?" Deven demands.

"I don't remember. It doesn't matter."

Jade the diplomat steps in. "Don't worry, Aunt Martha, toast and plain hot cocoa will be fine."

"Thank you so much, Jade," I say a bit more sarcastically than I intend, popping bread in the toaster, arranging the butter, cinnamon, and sugar. I fill the kettle. The kids rush to the china closet. "Hey, hey, wait a minute. No hands on the china." I reach back for some cups and saucers, the ones I could break without shedding a tear.

They reach for their own, constantly keeping me off balance.

"I'll get the napkins," Darren volunteers.

Deven's right behind. "I'll get the spoons."

"Aunt Martha, remember to cut them into four triangles," Jade says.

"NO!" Deven yells. "I want a *piece* of bread, no triangles!"

I rub his shoulder. "You can have it cut however you want, Deven."

Jade insists that he have it the "right way."

He starts to cry, and one of the cups and saucers that I don't care about hits the kitchen floor. I squat and wipe away his tears. My hands seem bigger all the time on his little face. "You can stand right next to me and tell me what you want. Okay?"

"Okay," he says, firmly facing Jade. In the end, of course, he wants it exactly how Jade described, but when Jade begins to hold it over his head, I give her the Look—the mad-mother-don't-make-another-move look. I'm out of practice, but actually, it still works quite well.

They're settled at the dining room table after a tortured discussion of who lights the candles and who adjusts the lighting in the chandelier.

Raina is in the living room, a Pepsi in one hand, her feet up on the coffee table, scouring a Pottery Barn catalogue. She looks so pleased at the opportunity of having a quiet moment that my resentment of the high-intensity evening visit melts away.

"Hey, give me the application," I whisper. She puts down the catalogue and tosses me the forms. "I'll copy these and you can bring them home. . . . You *are* going home tonight, right?"

She scans the results the hurricane of her children left in the living room before attacking the kitchen. She listens to the kids in the dining room and hears the happy chatter of "tea time." She looks at herself settled in—comfortable and immersed in the quiet, the soft pastels in the Pottery Barn catalogue, the stuff of dreams that may begin with a house. A Habitat house.

"Yes . . . I think we'll go home tonight." She returns to her browsing. "I'm not sure when though. . . ." She smiles.

I grab the new Ikea catalogue and tap her on the head with it.

In my run upstairs to my study I have a rush of optimism, not common for me.

Somehow I just know this is going to work.

THE VINEYARD, CONTINUED

The Grant family is officially accepted as a Habitat partner family. If Raina can get the sweat-equity hours in and fulfill the other obligations, they are guaranteed a three-bedroom house. Habitat, God bless them, even came to the hospital to meet with Raina to go over the details. They've also decided that Raina will have a house with a basement and a second bathroom in case Deven needs to be isolated from his siblings, if a home health care worker is needed at any point. They also promise to put in the special air filter the doctor has recommended.

It is such good news, but Raina is overwhelmed at everything she has to do in the midst of the nightmare she's currently living. However, when she's just about to lose it she imagines her brand-new house. I start saving the tons of catalogues that get stuffed through our mail slot. In the quiet moments, while Deven sleeps at the hospital or home, she flips through them for decorating ideas. She is tired all the time. She feels guilty all the time. The juggling game she's looking at alternates between a dream and an impossibility.

The Dollar Store

*A*nother Christmas, another shopping adventure with the kids.

This year, a dollar store has opened down the street, just like the ones in the Outer Banks of North Carolina, where we go on vacation with my family every May. Everything is a dollar. I love these stores. Floor to ceiling, aisles too close together, they are crammed with the greatest collection of stuff: hundreds of key chains that do everything but call your mother and pay your bills, every basic kitchen utensil possible—badly made and good for one meal's use, if you're lucky, a collection of toys that will deceive children into thinking they've hit the jackpot for about an hour, and ashtrays and paperweights made of small crustaceans. And then some marginally good deals like gift wrap, bows, mugs, and knee-highs by the bag. I'm not alone: the kids think the dollar store is the coolest place for gift buying.

Each kid gets six dollars to cover gifts for Mom, Grandma, each other, and an optional. Deven wants to get his mother something "beautiful," and goes directly for the "ladies clothing department"—contained in several large bins in the first row. I'm three aisles over with Jade when we hear him yell, "Aunt Martha, I found it! *And I can read.*"

I run over to see what he's talking about. He holds up a long red chiffon scarf with the words "Jesus Loves Me" in glittery gold letters all over it. All I can muster at first is, "Wow!"

"My mom will love it," he pronounces confidently.

"Oh yes, she will, Deven. It is a wonderful present. But how do you know how to read?"

He points to a word on the scarf and proclaims, "Jesus!"

"You're right." I pat him on the back. "You *do* know how to read."

Jade is in the next aisle, wanting to show off the frame she's chosen for her mom. It gets an A+ for tackiness, but Raina will never forget who gave it to her.

"Come here," Darren bellows from the back of the store. "I got the best one!"

"Really?" I yell back as I try to find him. I almost lose my lunch when I see what he's holding over his head. Unless I can think of some way to intervene, on Christmas morning in front of his entire extended family, his mother will open a lovely package with a beautiful blonde in a tropical setting and the words, *Summer's Eve Disposable Douche* above the picture. "Darren, honey, do you know what this is?"

"No, but isn't it nice?" he asks.

"Oh yeah."

Deven and Jade, who have joined us, agree.

"Darren," I say, "I just thought of something really important. You know sometimes stores keep some of these things on the shelf longer than they are allowed to. You always have to check the date on them to be sure." I make a big fuss of looking for the date and finally find a string of numbers. I show them to the kids very seriously and say, like I just discovered bugs in food, "It's a good thing we checked!"

Darren does not give up easily. The dollar store is overwhelmed with a stock of Summer's Eve disposable douches and he wants me to check the dates on other boxes. I draw the limit at five, adopt an expression suitable for a person inspecting for poisonous substances in baby food. With each box, I solemnly shake my head back and forth. We move on.

Darren, a resilient child, sets off to find a second choice, while Jade and Deven hunt for goodies for Grandma and each other. "Hey," yells Darren, "this is even better." He holds up a leopard-print thong that can't be more than a size 2—4 at the most. He's absolutely thrilled with his discovery, and there's no

way I'm talking him out of it even though he also got his
mother a thong for her last birthday. At least this one doesn't
have "Hey, Baby," written on it. He then announces that this
year, he's spending one dollar on a gift for his mother and five
dollars on himself. I lecture him on the true meaning of Christmas and the need to give of one's self to others, making absolutely no impression. But he knows that there's no way I'm
going to let him buy himself five dollars' worth of junk to keep.
So in his magnanimity he decides that Grandma needs an extremely noisy motorcycle windup toy and that Jade will love a
miniature red sports car with purple flames shooting across the
sides. Deven, he tries to convince me, has always longed for a
gruesome plastic beast with a knife in its fist. I only have so
much energy to reason with him. Most days I'd describe him as
persistent. Today he is just plain stubborn. And as he pays for
the stuff on his own at the cashier, he is also extremely happy.

Deven and Jade's gifts are almost as interesting. During the
ten-minute drive home I deliver the same lecture as last year.
"You will wait to give and open presents on the exact day of celebration. On Christmas." They torment me with the big "why"
question. I give a couple of standard, "Because it's the way
things are done. That's when everyone's expecting it." Then I
switch to, "Just promise me you'll save these till Christmas."

"O-kay!!!" they respond in unison, uttered in the same
tone as the forbidden "Shut up!"

Almost as fun as the shopping is the gift wrapping. There is
a two-year Christmas ritual, with little allowance for deviation.
With three full bags and three enthusiastic kids, we almost fall
through the door. "Plug in the Christmas tree. Put the music
on. Light the pinecone candles. Make the cocoa. Did you remember marshmallows?"

"One thing at a time." I try to slow them down. One child
helps me with each task.

As I begin to pour the cocoa into our everyday mugs, Jade stops me. "Aunt Martha, no . . . not those!" She walks over to the china cabinet and points to the good stuff. It's my grandmother's Spode china . . . no way. However, they can't tell the difference between that and a similar, far less expensive pattern I bought from Pier One to increase the number of table settings. Cups and saucers. If they break, they break. She finds the silver tray, a silver bowl for the marshmallows, cloth napkins, and a china plate for arranging the Christmas cookies.

Once we settle in, we open a cabinet full of jumbo rolls of wrapping paper, every piece of colored tissue paper I've ever been given, old bows, and other little goodies to make gifts interesting. It takes several hours and God knows how many rolls of tape to wrap the gifts. "Over the top" doesn't begin to describe the results. I give each child a large shopping bag and we write their names in huge letters on their bags—not that there would *ever* be any questions about which gifts were which, given the distinctly unique styles of each child.

Jade has obviously been giving some thought to the promise she made about restraining gift giving until Christmas, for she says solemnly, "Aunt Martha, my mom said it's bad to keep secrets."

"Well, Jade, there are good secrets and bad secrets, and not telling people about their presents is a *good* secret." She doesn't buy it for a minute.

Their mother isn't fully in the front door, and the twins have dragged their bags over to her and are already unwrapping their presents for her. She takes a quick peek, walks into the kitchen. Raina reaches into the refrigerator for a Pepsi and whispers to me, *"Another thong?"*

"Oh no, my friend." I laugh. "One of my presents to *you* is what I saved you from opening in front of your entire family on Christmas morning."

"What was it?" She takes a swig of Pepsi.

"A really, really lovely box of . . . Summer's Eve disposable douche."

Pepsi spurts in all directions.

I imitate her opening it on Christmas morning. We are like two giggly little kids. The noise draws the children to the kitchen, and they stare at us in confusion and bemusement.

"Why are you laughing?" they demand.

We have no answer. But I am aware of that precious part of my heart or mind responsible for pure happiness. Joy is definitely in the house.

ALL WHITE PEOPLE AREN'T ENGLISH, ESPECIALLY THE IRISH

Now that Jade is a first-grader, she's become more acutely aware of racial differences. She's studying other countries and adores geography and folktales. Any adult walking into this house would know from all the decorations that this is a home of people of Celtic origins. Jade and Brian have had multiple conversations about the Irish. The kids are spending this Saturday with us while Raina puts in her Habitat sweat equity hours. Brian is paying the bills in his study.

Jade walks excitedly to his door and announces, "I know what you are!"

"What am I?" he answers innocently.

"You're a English!" she pronounces with authority.

Brian recoils. An incredibly gentle man, he nonetheless sometimes gets so angry about the tormented history of the Irish at the hands of the English that he refers to them by the IRA nomenclature of "Brits." He proceeds to explain to Jade how horrible the English were to the Irish. He tells her all about the "troubles." She loves it, half because she loves having Brian to herself and half because she adores stories.

When he finishes, she wants clarification. "Was this real or a folktale? We're studying folktales."

"Well, the stuff about leprechauns and St. Patrick is probably more of a folktale, but all the troubles the Irish had before and after they came to this country—that's true."

"Okay, Uncle Brian, if you're not a English, then what are you? A Europe?"

"No, honey, I'm Irish."

"Is Aunt Martha?"

"Yes."

"Is Keara?"

"Yes."

"Is Miss Rachel and Mr. Greg?"

"You know what, Jade, pretty much everyone in our families comes from Ireland."

He tries to turn the tables. "And where are *you* from?" He's eager to see what else she's learned from her studies of other countries.

"Oh, I'm from Arlington," she answers matter-of-factly. He leaves it at that.

MY MOM'S BUILDIN' ME A HOUSE

The apartment is getting tighter and tighter. The place looks very much like when they moved in, except with twice the stuff. Tempers are short. Two big enemies are money and time. Disease is the one that overshadows them both. Raina is trying to get in her required hours of building at Habitat sites, get Deven to the doctors, have time for Jade, and give Darren some daily exposure to the wide open spaces in which he needs to let loose.

Every week we check in with our observations of the progress . . . the groundbreaking, pouring the foundations, framing, and many things we don't know how to name but know must go up or in. Raina is learning how to do things like put up drywall. Because friends and relatives can contribute time, Elizabeth and CeCe, Raina's niece, are racking up the hours, too. The kids still don't entirely understand what's happening, but they know—in the midst of something that is day-to-day difficult—that this is an enormous but happy undertaking.

Darren and I hit Home Depot for some new laundry baskets, electrical tape, and then some of those great things you never knew you needed until you saw them. It's macho heaven—all that lumber, those huge cranes transporting anything, the busy circular saws. Darren is more than impressed. I get him a $5.99 compact "junior" screwdriver, hammer, and drill, with the caveat that I can find us some wood and do some hammering, but to expect nothing in the drilling department.

"Don't worry," he reassures me, "I'll find someone smarter."

Oh Lord, I'm so relieved.

We endure the long Saturday line. When we finally reach the friendly cashier, she asks, "How are you today?"

With great pride he blurts out, "My mom's buildin' me a house."

"Wow!" She says to me, "Congratulations!"

"She's not my mom. She's just my aunt."

The cashier looks totally confounded and, frankly, quite relieved the transaction is coming to an end. I can't help it. I start to laugh as we leave the store.

"How come you're laughing?" he wants to know.

"Because, Darren, you are some piece of work."

"Hey, Aunt Martha. I know, next time let's get me a toolbox."

"Well, sweet boy, we'll just have to see." I chuckle.

My mom's buildin' me a house. Wow. These are the moments you dream about as a parent—when your child is bursting proud of you. The problem is that you rarely hear it from the mouth of your own kid.

ST. PATRICK'S DAY

*W*e're celebrating St. Patrick's Day with a big boiled dinner: corned beef, cabbage, potatoes, carrots, soda bread, and a wicked Bailey's Irish Cream chocolate cake for dessert. This year, Raina, Elizabeth, and the kids join us. The children are amazingly well schooled—thanks to Brian—in Irish history. Jade and Darren fight over the St. Patrick's Day fable. For some reason Darren has it in his head that St. Patrick *ate* all the snakes in Ireland. Jade counters, "No, Darren, he drove them out of Ireland!"

"How?" he challenges.

Totally sure of herself, she says, "In a van or a truck or something." Jade's tone suggests she just showed a hundred-point IQ advantage over him.

We catch up on Habitat—the progress of the building, the families they've met so far. When Raina mentions where different people come from, she says she thinks one of the families is African.

"Yuk," sputters Jade. "I hate Africans." It's one of those statements that just hangs in the air, waiting for something to reach up and make it disappear—definitely a tough one to back away from.

Elizabeth is silently fuming. Brian looks straight down and decides it would be a good time to ask if anyone wants seconds of soda bread.

Raina and I, our heads bowed, happen to catch each other's eyes. We quickly look down at the Irish platter, studying the arrangement of the carrots and potatoes to fight the strong urge to laugh. I get up to clear the table and start the coffee.

Jade is a pro at slowly pushing an issue until she elicits a reaction. "I do! I hate them! Really I do!"

Elizabeth gives her another stern look and dismisses further conversation on the topic. "We'll talk about it when we get home, Miss Jade," she says ominously.

A perfect time to serve the cake. It's no more than an annual occurrence that I try a new recipe from a newspaper or a magazine, and even less common that it's successful. This one is a true winner. Elizabeth, who is a great cook, gives her approval and pronounces it one of the best cakes she's ever had. She has seconds and I promise her a piece to bring home. "Can you get me a copy of the recipe?" she asks.

"Sure, it's somewhere in one of the piles on my desk."

As Raina and I wash the dishes, she tells me she has to get the recipe, too.

"It's based on Bailey's Irish Cream," I tell her.

"What *is* that?" she asks.

"Are you *serious*?" I can't believe she doesn't know Bailey's.

"Yeah."

"You know those couple of bottles in the bookcase in the dining room with the Irish decorations on it? A liqueur, I guess you would call it."

"There's *alcohol* in that cake?" She almost drops the plate she's drying.

"Yeah, I told you . . . Bailey's Irish Cream."

"Oh my God!" She stops working.

"What?"

"I can't believe this! *Don't tell my mother!*" she demands.

"What's the problem?" I am totally confused by her concern.

"You know how my mother feels about alcohol."

"Yeah—she doesn't drink any."

"Do you think that matters?" she asks, incredulous.

"Well, we can just tell her that the alcohol totally burns off in the baking. That's the truth, Raina."

"No! No! Don't say anything! And don't ever give her the recipe! Tell her you promised to save slices for your parents. Don't give her any to bring home."

"Don't worry. There's no way I'm going to have your mother worrying about Jade hating Africans *and* finding out she's a boozehound all in the same night."

A handful of soapy water takes flight toward me from the general direction of Raina.

THE CALM BEFORE

*F*or weeks Raina has been hoping to be able to visit a close friend in North Carolina. We've been holding our breaths. Will Deven be okay enough for her to go? Raina lays out all his meds, with the complexity of dosage and timing. There are lists of instructions, which she starts to go over and then realizes I know most of it. The kids have scattered to their corners of our house. Before his mother leaves, Deven is hanging on my skirt, pushing for a tea party. Darren has tracked Brian down to his computer in his study, full of questions about what guy stuff they are going to be doing. He would be halfway across the street to the park right now if we'd let him. Jade is under my desk, using all her energy to pull out the big black dress-up trunk for one of her fashion shows.

We try to remind them that we have a whole day and a half. It's not a concept they can really comprehend. There are corners and drawers in the house that over time have become theirs. The dress-up trunk or the arts and crafts box—where each kid has his or her own stapler and tape. There's Keara's dollhouse on top of the hall table that has a turning foundation and is filled with fancy furniture, dolls, cups and saucers—the works. By the end of any visit, Darren and Deven will have pulled chairs from my study, slid them up against the table, and rearranged the entire dollhouse. Their memory is amazing. It will not be at all unusual in a future visit for Darren to run downstairs, asking who moved the doll out of the third floor bedroom. Since I don't pass my time with the dollhouse anymore, it's most likely that the table has been knocked in cleaning, and the boys are always thrilled to solve the "Mystery of the Third-floor Doll."

The bottom drawer of Keara's dresser is their "extra clothes" place. A shelf in one of Keara's large bookcases holds her childhood books. The family room—to be honest, a not entirely redeemed basement—has shelves with toys from my private practice with children and videos. Another bottom dresser drawer holds all the forgotten clothes, toys, and stuff from previous visits. And in Brian's study is a big blue-mesh bag filled with sports equipment. The other beloved place—but certainly one not reserved for them—is the kitchen sink. They know which of the dining room chairs they are allowed to drag into the kitchen and precisely how they should be placed. Brian once hit a bonanza of sponges at a Jumbo discount store. Since the sink is divided in two, they cook, they clean, and they can take hours playing there.

Brian suggests that we work off a little energy at the park.

Jade helps me throw together some PBJs, fruit, juice packs, and chips. Then we fight the good fight about who is and isn't going to be warm enough and who really doesn't have to pee. Experience has taught me not to believe any of them on the peeing question, so under protest they make at least a cursory visit to the bathroom.

The park is one long empty expanse. The kids have a blast. Brian takes to the field with Darren and a soccer ball. They run and throw and whoop in delight. Surprisingly, Deven decides that he wants a piece of the action. I have to tell myself to stop worrying and leave him alone. He runs, gallops, and skips out to the field and does a great job of keeping up. Brian's confident deep laugh, Darren's hearty high-energy yelps, and Deven's continuous giggle become a song as he jostles and bounces with the guys. I am hearing music. I am hearing *give it all you've got*. And before I figure out whether to laugh or cry, it stops. Deven slows dramatically and turns to come back. I think I see him limp, but I dismiss it because he's trying to run in his precious cowboy boots. He is breathless and lands in my lap. I wrap my arms around him. He's starting to look like he has two black eyes. And his hearing is way off. He gets mad every time I say something and he doesn't hear the end of it.

We gather up the kids and head home. Jade and Darren do quiet things while Deven takes a long nap. To my surprise, he wakes up bouncy and ready for whatever we have planned. The bags under his eyes are still there, but he has no complaints.

We slow down the pace of the rest of the visit. A pizza dinner by candlelight with crystal and cloth napkins, with the chandelier's level of illumination always the source of three different opinions and adjustment. These are long dinners, with Brian telling more hilarious stories of his childhood, and the kids telling theirs. They adore "Remember when?," listening to us telling stories about when they were younger, and then spinning their own. So different from only a year ago when I was restraining someone in my lap, balancing my energy between preventing drops and spills and cleaning up when I failed. Dinner with three little kids was a contact sport. But not anymore.

Cleaning up is almost as long as dinner because they all want to pull the chairs to the sink and wash dishes. The fact that we have a dishwasher is of absolutely no interest. Fortunately, afterward, Brian has lots of videos and popcorn to keep them more quiet than usual. Everyone is allowed to sit on our bed—a big treat. They want to make cards for their mom, filling lots of time with the overgrown arts and crafts box. Deven retains his crankiness about his hearing—with everyone.

When Raina picks him up she can't believe Deven had been so active. She also has noticed the hearing problems and says that she'd been warned it could be a side effect of the treatment. He's due for tests next week.

BAD NEWS

Several days later the ring of the phone jostles me out of boredom at the computer.

Jesus, it's almost 11:00 P.M.

"Hello," I answer in an unwelcoming tone.

"It's me," Raina says softly. "Can I come by?"

Damn. I want to watch a video. I want to go to bed. I don't want to hang out with anyone.

But I so rarely get to see her alone anymore that I tell her to come right over. I go in search of the Pepsi stash I keep only for her. She would rather drink dirty creek water than my beloved

Diet Coke. I heat up leftover dinner on the chance she hasn't had a chance to eat yet.

When she gets here, she hugs me tight—too tight—and settles into the couch. I start to blather on about Pepsi and dinner.

"Martha," she interrupts me, "just sit down."

I sit in my rocking chair across from her.

Something is up, but for the life of me, I don't know what.

"Deven's relapsed." Just that. "Deven's relapsed."

For the second time in my life, I am lost at the end of a long tunnel with something at the other end that I can't quite grasp. I don't understand. I appreciate that it is important and am certain that I will hate it. But the tunnel is long, and the news is slow to reach me. Fourteen weeks into my second pregnancy—which had been absolutely healthy, the baby's strong heartbeat in evidence for several weeks—I lay staring at a sonogram screen while more and more professionals bustled around me with increasing interest and concern. But I didn't break a sweat. My poor obstetrician had to tell me five times "Your baby is dead" before I even began to get it. Hearing Raina's words "Deven's relapsed" gives me that same unreal, sick feeling.

She lists the details of the results.

"The neuroblastoma has metastasized to his bones, liver, brain, and bone marrow. It's even worse than before."

"Well, what . . . what . . . ?" I have lost words.

"They want to give him lots of chemo, and if they can clean up the bone marrow like they did before, they may try a third transplant."

All the medical words . . . we've been saying them so much for so long. It's like there's nothing to say.

"How are you doing?" I ask.

"My heart is breaking," she whispers, "but it's in the hands of the Lord. I believe Deven will be healed."

"But how can you know that?" Strange how you can ask someone such intimate questions at such seemingly inappropriate times. But the status of our relationship these days is that it's okay.

"He will either be healed here on Earth or he will be in the healing arms of the Lord in Heaven," she says softly. "And it's not up to me what kind of healing it will be."

"But when you pray, aren't you praying for him to live?"

"I'm asking for healing."

"Raina, you know how alienated I've felt from my church, but it still is my faith, and what we would pray for is the same thing. But I always get caught up in praying for a miracle or asking God to change His mind or outlining how I want things to turn out. I mean, it's not just me. Scripture is full of people praying like that."

"You may be spending so much energy telling God what to do that you're not listening for the answer."

There's a beat of slightly uncomfortable silence that ultimately can't be resisted.

"Well, wouldn't that be a first for me?" I blush.

She bursts out laughing. "I'm so glad you said that because a second after it was out of my mouth I wasn't sure I should have said it. . . . But you know what I mean."

"All right, all right, I catch your drift." I chuckle.

"How about dinner?" she asks.

"It's just Brian's spaghetti and salad."

"And a cold Pepsi?"

"Yeah."

"Perfect."

I nuke her dinner while she puts her feet up and her head back on the couch. When I carry it back to the living room she looks unsure about whether she'd rather sleep or eat. She tests the spaghetti and decides it's good enough to stay awake for.

We talk softly about what's next and how she's going to have to tell Deven.

"It looked like he was home free," I tell her, "or was I missing the signs?"

"No, he was doing great. It's just this cancer—it's so fast, so powerful."

After dinner she collects the mail-order catalogues I save for her by the front door. She likes to look at them while she's killing time, waiting at the hospital and various offices. Killing time. It's more like time is killing her. But she is so strong.

We hug, harder and longer than usual.

Through my tears I say, "I love you."

Her voice catches in her throat as she says, "I love you, too. Try to pray, Martha . . . just try."

"I will. I promise."

Before bed I try her method of reading suggested Scripture passages and praying, but I am haunted by visions of the little guy running in his cowboy boots and laughing with such abandon a couple of days ago and I can't stop crying.

My grandmother's strands of rosary beads are in my bedside drawer in a flowered, heart-shaped candy box. I choose my favorite and settle under the covers. The beauty of the Rosary for me is that, even though it's sort of an old lady thing to do—after being raised Catholic and attending Sunday school—it is a ritual I identify with childhood. The recitation of the same prayers over and over again has a calming effect. At the beginning of each decade, I ask for something specific: courage for Raina, ease of the treatments for Deven, soothing Darren's and Jade's loneliness and confusion, for the wisdom and persistence of his doctors. But at the end, I can't help myself. No sooner have I made the sign of the cross and kissed the small silver crucifix when an angry, frightened voice in my head blurts out, *Just heal him, damn it. How hard can that be?*

ANOTHER TWIST

*R*aina calls.

"Martha, the boys are asleep and I was thinking about coming over after I get Jade in bed. Is that okay?"

"Yeah. Are you all right?"

"That's a good question. I just have something I want to talk to you about."

"Okay. Come when you can."

An hour later, a tired Raina knocks on the door and then remains in my greeting embrace a little longer than usual.

"Pepsi?" I ask.

"Oh yeah," she agrees. "But I don't think that anything can wake me up."

"Was it a bad day with Deven?"

"Not worse than any other."

We sit down, me with my Diet Coke, her with her Pepsi. I want to pump her for information, but I know the best thing to do is to keep my mouth shut.

She takes a few sips and draws a deep breath.

"I'm pregnant."

Inside, my mind is exploding. *Holy shit! What! Four children! Deven and a baby?*

On the outside I remain quiet and wait for her to continue.

"Are you sure?" I ask tentatively.

"Oh, I'm sure," she says with resignation.

"Well, how are you feeling?"

"I can't believe it. How can I have a child in the middle of all this? It's not possible to have a baby with such a sick child. I don't know what I'm gonna do. I mean, I can't even think about it all, it's so huge."

She's quiet again.

"And I'm disappointed in myself. How could I be so care-less? How could I let this happen? What am I going to do?"

I know Raina is against abortion, so this is really not a question about what she's going to do about the pregnancy.

"I'm barely keeping my head above water on good days," she continues, "and bad days—well, you know."

"Does William know?"

"Yeah."

"What did he say?"

"He's happy. You know he's in his forties and he has no kids. The only good thing is that I've seen him so much with my kids and he's so good with them, not like their father, so I won't be alone in it."

"Does that help?"

"A little. But, you know, it's not that far in our relation-ship . . . and my trust in men is low."

"With good reason," I agree.

"There's this little part of me that's happy. You know, a new life in the middle of all this sickness and these trials, like maybe there's some blessing in it that I just don't understand yet."

"That's a nice way of putting it," I quip, then instantly re-gret it.

She laughs joylessly.

"Raina," I tell her, "what's done is done. It's lousy timing, but try not to beat yourself up over it."

"That's not so easy."

"I know. How will the people at church react?" I ask, knowing that her church is quite strict in many of its rules.

"I've been going there since I was fourteen and it's a very accepting place. I'd like to make an appointment with my bishop, but you know my schedule. Even if I make an appoint-ment, these days I can hardly ever keep it."

"Oh, Raina." I go over and put my arm around her. "You know we'll be here for you . . . and for the baby."

"Thanks. I know you will."

"How are you feeling?"

"Real tired. My appetite's okay, but I could fall asleep standing up."

"Are you getting any sleep?"

"What do you think?"

"Y'know Jade and Darren can come over here for a few hours while you catch a nap when Deven falls asleep. I don't feel the need to entertain them all the time, so it's no trouble. You've got to take care of yourself."

"I will. I have a doctor's appointment. I get Medicaid during the pregnancy. I'm just waiting for my documentation. I hope I can have Dr. Salinas again. She delivered Jade and the boys. I really like her."

Raina looks at her watch and can't believe how late it is. "Oh, I've got to go."

"Okay, well just let me know anything I can do. Raina, I know it seems overwhelming, but you'll get through it. You've got to ask for help wherever you can get it."

We hug hard and long.

"I'll call you tomorrow to arrange for some nap times."

It is hard to say good-bye.

My friend Meri Danquah—who wrote a moving book *Willow Weep for Me*, a memoir about the experience of an African American woman—said something that remained with me and has haunted me since Raina and I became friends.

"The one myth," she wrote, "I have had to endure my entire life is that of my supposed birthright to strength." A heavy burden.

One of those things that sounds a lot better than it really is.

THE WORST NEWS

*D*even is in Fairfax Hospital, with a tumor near his wind-pipe. Over the past two years, setbacks and relapses have become a normal part of life. Treatment, then remission, then relapse. The problem is that the time from treatment to relapse gets shorter and shorter. Now it feels like it overlaps. Deven's still feeling the side effects of the aggressive brain radiation . . . and now his windpipe is affected, which is very dangerous for his breathing. He's having scans this afternoon to find out how much the tumor is impeding his windpipe. Sounds like more chemo. The doctor mentions an experimental radiation program in Philadelphia. Raina is doubtful that more radiation will make a difference. She doesn't want another "waste of time," especially since this one would require Deven and her to be away for weeks at a time.

I tell her that at this point, even if it doesn't cure him it may improve his quality of life.

She wants her whole family to be able to go to the annual church picnic—a huge affair and one of the high points of the year for all of them. They get about a thousand people and have all kinds of food, swimming, hayrides, and activities for the kids. Darren starts summer school on Monday. I tell her that Brian and I want to be flies on the wall to see him tormenting some teacher with one "why" question after another.

She laughs, but, as usual lately, it is joyless. She is weary: hospital weary, pregnancy weary, uncertainty weary. We make a backup plan. If Deven's not released tomorrow, Brian and I will bring him an indoor picnic at the hospital, as well as a brand-new video. She agrees, remembering one year ago when he went into the hospital the day before the picnic. She starts to cry. "I feel like such a bad mother."

"Why, because you'd love to go to the church picnic instead of being at the hospital?"

"Yeah, I just feel so selfish."

"Raina, I am not bullshitting you—sorry, lying to you. You are one of the best mothers I have ever known. I truly don't know how I would have come close to doing what you've been doing. You're pulled in a million directions. I mean, c'mon, give yourself a break. That picnic has been important to you since you were young. You are not selfish. In fact, you could stand to be a little more selfish. Okay?"

"Okay. I'll call you when I know more."

It's 10:30 P.M. and the phone rings.

"We've been released," she says.

"That's great."

"But . . . some of the scans came back," she adds softly.

My chest is full of bricks and stones.

"It's in his brain—all over—behind his eyes, everywhere."

She tells me how Dr. Prescott, who initially was cool, if not brusque sometimes, was the one to get the scans. She said that from the look of the scans she can't believe Deven's not confined to bed, in agony, on constant morphine.

"I told Dr. Prescott Deven's not even complaining of a headache," she tells me, "but she said that won't last long." Raina goes through the options they discussed, none of them hopeful, none of them very good.

"How are you?" I finally ask her.

"I'm hurting."

There's all this noise behind her, like everyone is in total denial of the situation.

I start crying, deep sobbing, can't-catch-my-breath crying.

And she does, too.

It's in the crying that we say what we really know.

She tells me, "Dr. Prescott's eyes were full of tears, and she said her heart was breaking."

Dr. Prescott released Deven with a prescription for morphine. He goes back to the hospital on Sunday or Monday.

I sit at my desk and feel the fault line trace a deep crevice through my heart. I walk in to tell Brian. He's stretched out on the bed, looking at intricate pictures and diagrams depicting Vice President Cheney and his heart problems on the TV. Just looking at me he knows to turn it off. I tell him what Raina told me. He can't talk. I don't need a diagram to see the shape of his heart. "Videos," he says. "We have to get more videos for him." He puts his head in his hands. "That little guy . . . my little guy . . ."

A Swede

Keara is in love. Ordinarily I would be flat-out happy for her. But he's Swedish. Not in the way that she is ancestrally Irish. He *lives* in Sweden. She met him while his band was touring the East Coast and they hit it off immediately. In the three weeks he was in the area, they became serious enough to make plans for Keara to visit Sweden between semesters, meet his family and friends, continue the relationship.

When she called and told me I was less than enthusiastic. Knowing exactly why, she tells me, "Sweden's not that far away."

"Honey, have you looked at a map lately?"

"Mom, I really thought you'd be happy for me."

"Oh babe, I am. It's just so far."

"I'm only going for two weeks. I got a great deal to go directly from New York to Gothenburg where Per lives."

"Oh."

"Mo-om."

"What?"

"Don't worry."

"What if he's *the one*?"

"What if he is?"

"I'll have a bunch of blond grandchildren I can't understand."

"Don't you think you're getting ahead of yourself here?"

"Yes, I am. If I do it again, you have my permission to tell me to shut up. Now tell me all about it."

She does. Gothenburg sounds wonderful. My concerns about Per being "just" a member of a band were quieted when I find out he has another job "in computers," which is always vaguely reassuring to me, probably because I don't understand them.

After talking for an hour, I admit to her, "I admire you."

"Why?" She laughs.

"Because I never would have had the nerve to do something like that at your age . . . or now, for that matter."

"Well, I'll be home next week to get some of my warm stuff."

"Okay."

"Mom?"

"Yes, love?"

"Don't worry about me."

"That's my job."

"Yeah, but, you know, don't *worry*."

"I won't. We'll leave that to Dad."

"Deal."

The Great Big Sea

*O*ver time Brian has turned Darren on to Celtic music, specifically a band from Nova Scotia called Great Big Sea. Brian has all of their CDs. Darren heard them over and over on our vacation trip back and forth to Maine. I just pray he doesn't let loose and sing one of their songs to his mother or grandmother, because drinking and raising hell are such clear and frequently expressed themes in our musical heritage.

When Great Big Sea comes to Wolf Trap—the Washington area outdoor summer concert venue—Brian buys tickets for the three of us. Darren is thrilled and counts down the days. We pick him up, spiffy in a plaid shirt and khaki pants. He is thrilled with the amphitheater in the midst of the trees, the lights, the sound system. He is so excited, he can't sit still.

Finally the band takes the stage. The blinking lights, the smoke, the screaming music, the percussion so intense you can feel it vibrate in your body—all makes me remember how music is always so much better live. Darren is wide-eyed and throws his arm around Brian. Brian squats down to hear what Darren wants to say.

"Uncle Brian," he yells joyously over the rocking music, "I never knew they were *real!*"

I would dare anyone to stay still and seated once this band gets going. We dance, clap, stomp, and sing along. It's a great concert. Our only complaint is that it doesn't last long enough.

As we make the long trek back to the parking lot, Darren clasps Brian's hand, and the two of them share their favorite songs. As we wait for Brian to unlock the van, Darren turns to me and says, "This is you." He does an imitation of me dancing at the concert. It is not flattering. There's no way to describe it except that it is just awful.

I laugh, but still protect my honor. "I don't dance like *that*."

"Aunt Martha, you dance like a white lady."

"Honey, I *am* a white lady."

"You *are*?" he asks, clearly surprised.

"Yes, I am."

"Is Uncle Brian?" His tone suggests he hopes the answer is no.

"Yes. Uncle Brian is white."

"Oh."

He's buckled into the backseat, and it takes us a while to break free from the long line of traffic leading out of Wolf Trap. Brian has a Great Big Sea CD on. He sings along, but Darren, who usually jumps right in, is silent.

As we finally get out on the open road, we hear his voice from the back, trying to be heard over the music. "Hey, hey."

Brian turns off the music. "Yeah, pal?"

"Uncle Brian?" he asks with great concern. "How can you, and Aunt Martha and Keara be in our family if you're all so white?"

I'm glad it's dark because I have a silly, stupid look on my face. But Brian doesn't miss a beat. *"That's because your family adopted us."*

"We did?"

"Yeah, you did."

"Oh okay," he answers, perfectly pleased with the response. I squeeze Brian's hand. I love him like crazy.

THE LITTLE FLOWER

*J*t's been a month since Brian's mother, Jane Mackay De-penbrock, died. And today is her birthday. She would have been eighty-one. Practicality demands that we shift from quiet mourning into action. We need to clean and clear and sort more of her property into categories ranging from hidden treasures to absolute junk.

She had already pared down so much to make the move from her four-bedroom house to the one-bedroom apartment built to adjoin her daughter, Janet's, house. It was a wonderful arrangement for ten years, until dementia—the great opportunist—claimed too much of her brain for independence, beyond what my sister-in-law, a nurse and generous daughter, could provide. There was complete agreement that she required twenty-four-hour care.

The big stuff had already been distributed among her four children—furniture, rugs, silver, her collection of Waterford crystal from her trips to Ireland. Most of what was left for us were boxes of small things—Madame Alexander dolls, photographs, and paper, paper, paper. I position myself on the floor and begin sorting by sibling—Brian, Janet, Tom, and John—for them to go through at home. Brian's family is very funny, and every little thing from someone's paper trail will launch one of them into some memory that quickly has us all laughing.

During one of the pauses, I notice something simultaneously familiar and foreign on top of the far corner of Jane's dresser. It is a statue of St. Thérèse de Lisieux, otherwise known as the Little Flower of Jesus. It's an old plaster statue about sixteen inches high, all banged up. Jane had this statue since childhood. The story goes that when she was five, she developed a life-threatening pneumonia. She was encased in an iron lung when a family friend brought a tiny relic of St. Thérèse, pressed it to her, and within several days, Jane was completely healed. The practice of relics is often hard for people who aren't Catholic — and many who are — to understand. To treasure the tiny piece of bone encased in glass attached to your rosary beads or in a locket around your neck requires that you not give too much thought to how it got there. But there are thousands of stories of healing from the use of relics, and Jane's is one of them.

Of all the saints, I chose Thérèse as my childhood patron. As soon as I could read, my grandmother enrolled me in the Saint-of-the-Month book club. I was only interested in the girls, and Thérèse especially captured my imagination. She had been an incredibly devoted and determined girl who wanted to enter the convent much earlier than the approved age of admission. She refused to take no for an answer. While on a pilgrimage with her father, fifteen-year-old Thérèse came right out and asked Pope Leo XIII to override the age requirement. He denied her request on the spot, but by the end of that year, she was a Carmelite nun.

I loved the fact that *nothing* was too mundane for her. She believed that the most ordinary things were potentially the most sacred. Somehow I got that as a child, and then lost it in my adulthood. She was strong willed, but physically frail, and she died of tuberculosis at the age of twenty-four.

Thérèse is always depicted the same way — in a chocolate-brown habit with a white scapular, a cream-colored cape draped over her shoulders, falling in rich folds to her feet. She holds a large crucifix, arms filled with roses. Her eyes are blue, serene, and slightly sad; and she has long graceful hands and fingers.

My grandmother had the same statue in the creepy fourth floor bedroom I used to sleep in when I visited her in Massachusetts. I loved to dust it off and bring it into bed with me. This was in pre-Barbie days, when dolls were rarely grownups. I knew nothing about Thérèse then. So I made up a number of totally inappropriate, possibly sacrilegious but innocent adventures for her—with themes, closer to *The Patty Duke Show* than anything from *Lives of the Saints*.

But it started us off on firm footing.

I prayed to her in the litany of nighttime prayers. She was the one I turned to for the big stuff: "Saint Thérèse, please stop the fight my parents are having. Please don't let my mother have more kids. Please stop my father's drinking. Please stop Sister Mary Alphonse from pulling my hair. Please make my handwriting better so I don't have to practice with the boys at recess." I took her at her word that nothing was too ordinary, although I'm fairly sure I missed a little of her meaning at the time.

I tended not to make a lot of deals with God. That's one of the great things about Catholicism: you can "dial direct" if you want or you have all these people who can intercede for you, like playing up to your father for something you know your mother would forbid. I preferred working through the female saints closer to my own age. I'd make deals with them, and, let's face it, I didn't have a lot of bargaining chips on my side—except desire and need.

At the time I was convinced that my best thing I had to bargain with was the choice of my confirmation name. I would receive the sacrament of confirmation, in which I would become a full-fledged member of the church, when I turned ten. As a symbol of my elevation into spiritual "adulthood," I would be allowed to adopt a saint's name that would become part of my own. I treated the promise like it was some big prize in the spiritual arsenal. Some eight-year-old pain in the ass in Merrick, New York, who was planning to honor a saint by the world-shaking sacrifice of interrupting the perfect alliteration of her name—MMM: Martha Mary Manning.

From a pragmatic perspective, it was never a good oath, never a smart bet. My grandmother's name is Mildred, and as the oldest grandchild I had the first shot at the big payout. It would be so easy. I could just add Mildred to the string of *M*s. But smarmy Martha was bad enough. Martha and Mildred seemed like a guarantee of spinsterhood, even from the perspective of a ten-year-old. When it came right down to it, I couldn't compound my parents' poor judgment with my great-grandmother's. I adored my grandmother Mildred, but I had limits. (Of course, my sisters came along and, being no fools, acted like perfect suck ups and hit the jackpot when they adopted her name, leading my brother to take the saintly name of Harold just because my beloved grandfather had deep pockets when he was happy.)

I admit to brief flirtations with a couple of others—St. Bernadette, St. Catherine—but I always returned to my girl Thérèse. Many classmates were taking her name but they Anglicized it to the wimpy Theresa. With a tremendous sense of pride—the kind that's a sin—I claimed her real name, in her native language. The bishop would have to do that French gurgle in the back of his throat as he slapped me on the cheek and welcomed me into the Army of Christ.

My mother-in-law's statue was slated for the trash. Though I was tempted to take it, I was embarrassed to ask. Its size hindered my just slipping it out in my purse. How do I explain my connection to it? Do I confess to the collection of my grandmother's rosary beads in my bedside table drawer? That lately

I've been pulling them out more and more—regressing to one of the earliest forms of prayer I've known? It's rote, meditative, tactile. I tell no one. All I say is that I'd like to see if I can fix her up, restore her somehow.

Once I get her home, she becomes a paperweight in the corner of my disaster of a desk.

I am so tired. I miss my mother-in-law, her unconditional love for me since I was sixteen, her capacity to live in the moment, go with the flow, milk any ounce of enjoyment out of the most ordinary situations. So different from me.

I ache all over. Tomorrow is D day, Deven-at-the-doctor day. Just complaining to myself about my weariness makes me feel guilty as I automatically compare myself to Raina. It's not the feeling a few good nights' sleep will help. It's long-haul exhaustion: emotional more than physical. I sit at my desk, returning calls, checking e-mail, working at the computer, but I feel so sad.

Raina and I are separated somewhat by the thing that's supposed to draw people together: religion, faith, spirituality. It's not something I can reason my way into and out of. We are at the heart of the questions. What do you pray for? What do you believe God can or will do in the face of your prayers? It hurts that I have neither the intellectual understanding nor the unshakable faith to grasp this. I can't make Deven better. I can't take this burden from Raina. My prayers are fragmented. They are the words of the eight-year-old me, with similarly empty promises. I start to cry . . . sitting at my desk that will take days to clear, with St. Thérèse presiding over the chaos.

Through my tears, I lean over and bring her to me, taking a full inventory of her many insults and injuries. The tip of her nose is broken off. There are dents in her lovely cream cape. The dark-brown habit is badly chipped. The roses have lost most of their color. The crucifix is battered. Parts of Thérèse's face are colorless, one of her lovely eyes is almost wiped out.

I grab a marker and a couple of types of glue and begin to fill in the holes in her cloak. It goes so well that from a bit of distance, I can't really see the original injuries. It gives me hope to go on to the harder stuff. I get my box of old paints and my makeup case and blend colors till I get a match with the cream-colored habit. A little more experimentation and I restore both her pale complexion and the slight blush in her cheeks. Her poor eye takes a great deal of detail, but, by now, I am on a mission. Each broken, banged-up, or lost part that I repair energizes me, gives me hope that I can really fix her. The crucifix goes quite easily. I take an emery board and smooth the gorgeous cascade of roses and then mix different shades of red to give them dimension. I find a gold leaf pen and go a bit over the top highlighting some of the roses.

For two hours I lose myself in St. Thérèse. Nothing exists outside my mission to restore her. She would call this a prayer. I'm not so sure. But it occurs to me that I wasn't really restoring St. Thérèse just now. Reaching way back to my childhood, I think she was restoring me.

KEARA IN SWEDEN

The nice, though expensive, thing about Keara is that when she was a little girl she really took those phone company ads that said "Reach out and touch someone" to heart. Wherever she is, she reaches out and touches us. And, frankly, damn the cost. From her calls home, Keara has all the makings of an expatriate. She is having a blast in Sweden and is clearly even more in love with Per. She has met his mother and stepfather, his father, his siblings, and friends. She adores Gothenburg, delighting in the long warm days, and is picking up a little Swedish here and there. I even talk to Per, whose English is letter-perfect. He sounds like a lovely guy, except, of course, that he's Swedish and has no great desire to make the United States his home. After she's seen Gothenburg, I can hear in Keara's voice the fact that she could easily move there. I try to keep those little blond Swedish-speaking grandchildren out of my head when I talk to her, because she is clearly so happy.

"When do you come back?" I asked gently.

"Four days," she answers miserably.

"Honey, you can always go back."

"Well, luckily Per's band has another East Coast tour in two months."

"That's good."

Then the bomb.

"And, Mom, I already called Dad at work and told him. I'm going to look into studying for a year in Sweden."

"Do you think they'll let you?"

"I don't really care. I'll take time off if I have to. They're very open about letting people like me take courses."

"Oh. Well that's — " I get a little sniffly.

"Mom?"

"Yeah?"

"It's okay."

"Oh, honey, I know that. You just have to let me have my mother-bird feelings. I'm happy for you."

"And when Per comes to New York, we're going to come to D.C. so he can meet you and Dad."

"It will be really nice to have a person to connect with his name. I can't wait to meet him."

"Mom, I've got to go. We're going to Per's mom's for dinner. You'd love her."

"Okay. Call before you leave so I can worry."

"Yeah, yeah, yeah. Love you."

"Love you, too, sweet girl."

THE DECISION

*D*even does well with the additional chemotherapy cycles. He is an amazingly resilient boy. Even though he is small for his age, there is such sturdiness to him and unlimited enthusiasm for life. The information on his chart doesn't jibe with the kid I see in front of me. He may be sick, but he is not a sick kid, not to himself, not to his brother and sister.

For several months Raina and the oncologists have been weighing the future. With the extra stem cells they have in reserve, the doctors want to go ahead with a third and perhaps a fourth transplant. They tell Raina they can wait a little while before starting the chemotherapy in the hospital again. Raina has major doubts. She considers several experimental protocols. She has been warned that with each transplant Deven's system experiences more wear and tear, increasing his chances of succumbing to organ failures. She remembers the fevers, the vomiting, the mouth ulcers, and the many other agonies, and tries to balance it against his chances for a cure. The doctors say that with continued chemotherapy only, he can probably sustain "quality of life" for six months to a year. She decides to find her answer in prayer.

AT THE KITCHEN SINK

*I*t's the phone. I swear the sun hasn't come up yet. Brian grumbles in his sleep and turns over. I grope for the receiver and struggle to get the right end to my ear. "Hullo?" I mutter thickly.

A little voice chirps, "Hi, Aunt Martha. I was thinking that I don't have anywhere to go today so it would be a good idea for me to come over. What do you think?"

"Deven?" I stumble in my sleep. "What time is it?"

"It's morning."

"Never mind. Honey, did you call me *yourself*?"

"Yeah. I pressed the button," he answers with pride.

"Well, does Mommy know you're calling me?" I start to wake up.

"Not yet."

"Where is Mommy?"

"Sleeping."

"Listen, love, it is morning, but *early, early, early* morning. When Mommy wakes up—and, Deven, *don't wake her up*—call me back. If she says you can come over, it's okay with me."

"Okay. I'll call you in a while."

"Deven, don't call me in a *while*. Have Mommy call me *after* she wakes up . . . *on her own*."

"Okay. Bye."

I get a good look at the clock. *Good God, it's 5:15.*

Raina calls at 8:30. "Did you get a call this morning?" she asks, chuckling.

"Did he really do it on his own?" I ask.

"I guess so. He got good at it in the hospital."

"When he always called from there, I thought a nurse had dialed for him."

In the background I can hear him pestering, "I told you so," and "Can I go? What did she say?"

"Mr. Deven has learned a lot," Raina marvels.

"I guess so. Did he tell you about his plans?"

Raina laughs. "He knows exactly the plans. He is coming to your house as soon as possible and staying as long as he feels like it."

"I told him he could come over. What's the story with the other guys?"

"They're going to be very unhappy, but, Martha, it's a day he feels good, he's not totally attached to me, and I feel like he should have some time alone. You can do things at his pace —"

"Oh boy, they're going to be pissed."

"He's missed out on a lot of time with you they've had. It will be okay."

"Can I sleep over?" I hear him ask. Jade's and Darren's questioning voices are beginning to rise in the background.

"Raina, I'd love to have him sleep over, but we should probably play it by ear, given how he feels . . . and I have to get up to speed on the new meds."

"Okay. Let me put him on the phone."

"Aunt Martha, am I coming over? Are you gonna let me sleep over?"

"Yes, you can come over and if you feel okay you can sleep over. But the thing is, Deven, you really have to help me with all your meds."

"Okay, but the one thing is that I need to sleep in your bed." *Yeah. So what else is new?* "Uncle Brian will have to sleep someplace else."

"Oh, well, we'll have to let him know."

"It's okay. He'll be okay," he says with great confidence.

"Do you want me to pick you up?"

"Yeah, hurry. I already packed my suitcase."

"It'll be about twenty minutes."

"Is that more than an hour?"

"No, much less. Mom needs time to put together your meds."

"Okay, but after you pick me up, can we get Nuggets?"

"Yeah, then I thought we could stop by the video store, so start thinking about what you want to watch."

I can't wait to have a happy, healthy Deven to myself for a whole day and night if all goes well. But I brace myself for the storm that awaits me when I show up to pick up just one child instead of all three.

Darren meets me at the door. He is furious. Before I get a word out, he yells tearfully, "It's not fair!" I try to explain the fact that Deven and I are making up for lost time. He's not buying it. "You love him like he's your son!" he screams. I can't get a word in. "And he has a bald head and I have bushy hair."

"Darren, remember how you came on vacation with us for two weeks all by yourself?"

Jade jumps right in, over my question. "And he gets all the attention because he's sick!"

They are both crying and I feel so low.

"But, guys, remember that we're going to the movies tomorrow. I haven't forgotten it."

Darren hits the wall with his fist. "I hate tomorrow!"

"Darren, I promise you will have your time." He turns his back to me.

Deven has the tiniest of smiles on his face. If it were any broader he'd be taunting *Nah-nah, nah-nah, nah!* "C'mon," he says. "We have to go."

Raina stops him. "Deven, what have you got there?"

He proudly holds up a backpack and another bag.

"I packed the backpack with everything you need, Deven," she tells him.

"No, I need this stuff, too," he insists.

Raina throws up her hands. "Whatever, Deven . . . You can show it to Aunt Martha when you get to her house."

He pulls the backpack over a shoulder, indicates that I should take the athletic bag that contains God knows what, and announces resolutely, "Well, bye. We have to go. There's a lot to do." He is rubbing it in to two very unhappy siblings, who probably still won't be happy with me after the promised movie and junk lunch expedition tomorrow. I'm glad Raina is there with them, because she understands the degree of anger and where it's coming from, while many other relatives see it as pure selfishness.

Deven has constructed an impossible eighteen hours that I'm fairly sure his body will resist long before I do. When we get to my house, we unpack his meds and divide them into refrigerated and room temperature. I tape Raina's list to the wall. His clothes are folded like they were just bought at the Gap. Raina's disapproval of my more casual approach to cleaning and folding laundry continues to earn her my teasing title of Laundry Nazi, half because she's made it clear that it's really "all right" if I *don't* do the kids' laundry, and also because I admit I've tried and my laundry never comes out looking like hers.

Deven is less interested in showing me his mother's choices and much more into his own. He makes me sit down while he demonstrates everything in that bag. A *Blue's Clues* towel and game, at least five *Barney* and *Veggie Tales* videos, several of the play hats that Brian bought him, a coloring book, his cowboy boots, and his church clothes.

All in all, he looks pretty good—if you don't lift up his shirt to see the port for all the meds inserted in his little chest or roll up his sleeves to see the deep bruises or know exactly how old he really is. His bald head is growing downy, straight hair. I call it baby-chick hair. It is still a source of consternation to

him, since he continues to insist that each time he's gone bald
it's been the result of his mother sneaking into his room at night
and cutting all his hair off.

"Well, I guess we have a lot to do," I tell him.

"Can I see the dollhouse?"

"Yeah. Can you drag the chair over yourself?"

"I need help."

So I bring the chair over, and he gives an entire critique of
the changes. And he knows the culprits—Jade, Darren, and
Rachel's children, Tori, Gracie, and Sean. Tori has still not sur-
mounted her fears that our house is not haunted by the evil organ
in *Beauty and the Beast*. The two families of children have gotten
to know each other in day visits, usually to each other's family
parties. Tori's fears have turned out to be contagious among her
siblings, so most of the prints are Darren and Jade's.

Deven wants a full accounting of whoever has been near it,
which I can't provide. As momentary king of the house, he calls
me into my study and has me type up a note, saying "Leave this
dollhouse alone. Don't move anything. Thank you from Deven
Grant, age five." We tape it on the dollhouse and he's headed
for the kitchen and on to the next ritual he loves.

When he turns to get down from the chair, he notices writing on the wall at the top of the stairs. "Who wrote on the
wall?" he demands like he's the house monitor.

"I did," I confess.

"But you're not allowed."

We get up close to the writing.

"I am allowed for this writing. It's something we did since
Keara was little. Every now and then she stood against some
wall and we drew a line at how tall she was, and then we'd
write the date and how old she was."

"Why?"

"So we could remember her at different ages."

"How old was she at this one?" His finger traces one of lines.
"Let's see. She was seven."

He stands beneath the line and wants me to compare his
height to hers. "Do me. I want mine here. We can see how
much I grow."

I got a ruler and pencil from my study. He stands like a little soldier at attention while I place the ruler on top of his head
and draw his height on the wall.

"Write Deven—five years old and . . . what's the *day*?"

"July 8, 2001."

We stand there and admire it for a few seconds until he
gets us back on his schedule. "Let's cook."

"Should we *real* cook or *play* cook?" I need clarification.

"We'll real cook later before Uncle Brian gets home and
surprise him, but let's play cook."

Play cooking is a very old activity with the boys. At almost
three, Jade went right to simple, real cooking—muffins, ba-
nana bread, frosting cakes. But the boys started out sitting on
the kitchen floor, like Keara used to do, with plastic measuring
cups, long spoons, and other utensils.

When they turned two they demanded to stand at the sink
like grown-ups. Things became more complicated: monitoring
them both standing on chairs and making sure they understood
that water temperature was still my responsibility for another
year. Pure water and lots of imagination lost their appeal after a
while. From then on we used " 'gredients," leading to some of
the most disgusting concoctions I've known.

They started off equally equipped with bowls and utensils
each at his own sink. Then I started sweeping through my cabinets, drawers, and refrigerator for food that no one would eat,
because it was old or just plain disgusting. I cleaned out from the
refrigerator nearly empty containers of fruit juices and yogurt
just past its due date. They each got old boxes of cherry Jell-O

and butterscotch pudding. There were olives, powdered soup, oatmeal, stale Cheerios, tea bags, coffee grounds, a little food coloring, and a package of imitation chicken gravy that has been in the same position on the same shelf since we moved in. To begin to teach them modulation, I took out a couple of large spice containers, like oregano and cinnamon, and introduced the concept of using tablespoons to measure. When Uncle Brian was doing the real cooking, he actually let them add specified amounts and they did quite well—and they loved it.

Deven opens containers. He hums while he measures and mixes. Every now and then he looks through the window and spots the cardinal that chooses our humble backyard to settle in every summer. When we're really lucky, a bird so blue I swear it's a decoy, also flirts around the corners. I am not usually overcome by a love of nature, but every time I see one of them there is a mandatory cessation of whatever I'm doing just to watch the Wild Kingdom—by neglect, not design—of our backyard. Deven is equally impressed, and whenever he sees them, he dramatically points, using a utensil dripping with food in its loosest definition, splattering it liberally all over the kitchen.

He sings, he stirs, and he offers me pretend tastes. It is often at these times, when a child is side by side with a grown-up—not head-on, but when they are both sharing an activity— that the really interesting stuff gets said.

From out of nowhere he says, "My mom said I never have to be afraid 'cause God always walks behind me."

I don't know what to say.

"Does God walk behind you?" he asks.

I still don't know what to say.

He nods forcefully. "Yeah, yeah. He does," resolutely answering his own question.

Deven makes a few more incredible food combinations and tells me, "Sometimes I miss my mommy so much. And when I was all alone in the hospital, it was so bad, and I love my mommy, and when I grow up, I still want to be with her all the time. And you know what Mommy said to me? She said that no matter where she is, I am always in her heart."

I really have to focus on the disgusting concoction to keep from crying.

"Your mom loves you *so* much," I reply.

He sprinkles paprika over what is now a purple-brown ooze and adds, "And Darren, too . . . and Jade."

"Uh-huh," I agree.

Standing on the chair we are head to head. He takes my face in his hands like he used to do when he was little and asks sweetly, "Aunt Martha?"

"Yes, honey?"

"Are you still having all that work done on your teeth?"

"Yes, I am."

"I thought so," he replies casually as he returns to his mixture.

"Why?" I ask, out of general curiosity.

"Oh, just 'cause your breath is still kinda bad."

PER

*K*eara's boyfriend, Per, travels from Sweden to New York with his band, Girlfriends, for another East Coast tour. Keara brings him to North Carolina, where my extended family has gathered for our annual week's vacation. He and she are quite brave to take the whole family on at the same time. But he is sweet and gracious, able to shoot the breeze with the women and equally comfortable with the men. Keara brushes me off when I tell her he is very good-looking, but later in the night she whispers in my ear, "He is, isn't he?"

It is clear they are very attached to each other. Keara lets us know that she has made up her mind. She is going to Gothenburg to live with Per, see where the relationship goes, and learn as much as she can about Swedish history and culture. For some unknown reason, Brian and I are much calmer about it than I would have imagined. Probably because there isn't a damn thing we can do about it. She will leave in July, after spending a month at home, gathering all the things she needs to bring. There is no unit of measurement to describe how much I will miss her.

Waiting for the Cable Guy

*R*aina has to go out to consolidate some medical benefits for Deven's treatment. I have a hungover feeling from the cocktail of mood stabilizers and antidepressants. I took it too late and then woke up too early. I am tired down to my bones. But I couldn't cry if I wanted to.

The cable guy is supposed to come over. Brian and I want Deven to be able to get the shows that he enjoyed in the hospital. Some of the characters, like Blue, he came to love.

Deven is sitting back in the recliner, watching a video. Jade is off the wall. I don't know if it's me or her, but she can bother me in way that makes me want to scream. I never mind Deven and Darren crawling all over me—and their hugs are usually full-body high-energy-affection assaults. Darren hangs on me with his hand on my shoulder. Jade's is more of a full body, all weight, never-ending body *hang*. The more you give her, the more she demands. She is incredibly whiny, instantly forgetting something I've just done for her.

"Jade, I just read you a book ten minutes ago."

"Oh yeah, but it was a *short* book, a *boring* book, a *baby* book."

I feel rage toward her and then instantly guilty about it. I realize that I remind this seven-year-old of the obvious—that she's the oldest and that I treat her as even older because, for her age, she is bigger and smarter than average.

She is always hungry—or as she says, dramatically, "starving"—surveying the kitchen as if she is on some competitive, timed treasure hunt. When I tell her not to touch the play hats that Brian got for Deven, she whines, "He's such a baby."

I want to throw her into a time-out. But a time-out for what? Acting like a baby, always needy, always on the lookout for signs that there will be even less for her than there is right now? For being angry and showing it? Jade is picking up a lot on the family Richter scale, but we never have time to help her interpret it, validate it, and give a *Wow! Those are some mighty big cracks! How does it feel when the earth shakes under you like that?*

Somehow Darren, who is louder and more active and physically all over the place, is easier to deal with. But, lately, I'm losing my patience even with him. He starts messing with a pile of arts and crafts materials he knows I've set aside for Jade. He has no interest in *creating* anything but a scene with his sister.

I yell, "Darren, leave that stuff alone. It's for Jade's project."

His hands hover ominously close to a tray filled with string and beads that will make a huge mess if they just happen to take flight.

"Did you hear me?" I demand with a shrillness in my voice that I hate.

He moves closer to inflicting chaos.

"Darren, I swear, if you touch that, I'm gonna . . ."

He stops and waits.

"I'm gonna smack you."

He smiles broadly because he knows he's got me.

"Aunt Martha, sometimes you yell, but you *never* hit kids. It's your *policy.*"

He cracks me up. Of course he has heard this a thousand times from me. "All right, you know I would never hit you. But you know what I mean."

"I'm buggin' you."

"Yeah."

He gives me a very exaggerated, "I'm *ðorrrrry!*"

Darren wants his playmate back.

At this point he wants any playmate he can get, so we push miniature cars over a racetrack we assemble together. The goal is to get the car to the end without crashing (even if crashing gets you to the end faster). There's a metaphor somewhere here, but I'm too tired to figure it out.

The cable guy calls and now says he'll be coming between 12 and 3. I hate him. I have to break the news to the kids, who put the blame squarely on me. Deven ignores the collection of hats Brian bought him—a wizard hat, a cowboy hat, a black derby with a silk band, a top hat. But I can tell when someone touches the wizard's hat—blue velvet with gold stars—since he screams to put it back, that he likes it, at least enough for a momentary roar.

Jade brings down a big-girl book—a long one. She wants so much to be a little girl and sit on my lap, but it doesn't work like that anymore. She doesn't fit. Rather than give my tired "personal space" speech, I find a place for us to make a "comfy corner" with a couple of big pillows. We sit next to each other, and she settles in so that I can read and put my arm around her. Now it is *her* time. Nobody else's. No stopping reading because a younger kid doesn't understand the words. My back is killing me. It's hot. But Jade and I are back in sync. She lets out a long sigh and says, "This is just what I wanted."

"I'm sorry you didn't get it sooner, sweetie."

"Oh, that's okay. I love you, Aunt Martha."

"Jade, I know I can be really cranky, but you know I love you, too, right?"

"Yep," she says. "Keep reading."

Raina arrives home and tries to interest Deven in some cereal. He's at that perfect point of pain control with the least amount of sleepy side effects. He sits right up and starts going through the hats.

He tries on the derby, tilts it to the side, and mugs in his usual way. "Was this Uncle Brian's favorite hat?" he asks.

"Um, let me think. . . . Well, there was that pirate hat. Remember how you both got pirate hats? He loved that one."

"I did, too . . . and Darren," he agrees. "But which one is Uncle Brian's favorite *now*?" He still has the derby on, the one that sums up his "personality." I know what he wants me to say.

"Oh, he wanted you to know that the *derby*, the one you have on, is his favorite. He wanted to get one for himself, but it wouldn't fit."

"Because he has a bald head?" he asks totally seriously.

"I think it was a problem with size. They were all too small. What's your favorite?" I ask him.

"Uncle Brian's."

I nod.

"But, Aunt Martha?"

"Yeah?"

"I'm keepin' 'em all."

GREEN GABLES

*I*t's Jade's night to have an "alone sleep over," I'd been promising to show her one of Keara's and my all-time favorite movies, *Anne of Green Gables*, the story of an orphan girl and her adventures growing up on Prince Edward Island, Canada. It's a classic, but a lot of American girls don't know it.

We order a pizza and I let her have one soda—no caffeine. It's already 7:00 P.M. and I'm no fool. Jade needs a hit of caffeine like I need another doughnut. Watching anything with her is a test of patience. She has the notion, no matter what the movie is about, that the adult in the room has already seen it and knows *exactly* what's coming next and why. We hardly pass the introductory credits when she starts.

"Who's that? What's going to happen? Where's Anne? What's Green Gables, anyway?"

To me, movie watching is close to church in terms of the level of silence required of the attendees. For Jade, it's an interactive sport. The other major difference between Jade and me is the issue of what we've come to call "personal space." Jade loves to lean, bend, move my body around like a rag doll. It drives me crazy. She is a sweetheart, a love of a child who doesn't get people to warm to her as easily as they do to her brothers. Competing with those two is no small task. For the first year I knew her, she and I did things alone, and then, probably all of a sudden to her, it started to be a foursome. That must have felt like being shut out to her. And for the past two and half years, her life has been difficult. She hasn't had nearly the time and attention she wants or needs. Because she is so smart, I think people (including me) expect too much understanding and adapting to all the changes that have happened as a result of Deven's illness.

Brian is working late, so we get settled in on my bed. We snuggle under a puffy quilt—each with our own pillows (me and my personal-space rules). She lets out an audible sigh of comfort and delight. "It's just us girls." She smiles widely.

The video starts and she turns to me. "Aunt Martha?"

"Yeah?"

"I have to ask you a question."

"Is it important?"

"Yes," she says, knowing how I much I prefer silence with my movies.

"Okay," I say tersely.

"Okay, well here it is. . . . I don't know how to sew."

"Is that your question?"

"Yeah. Do you know how to sew?"

"Jade, *we're watching a movie.*"

"I know, but I just wanted to ask you about it."

"All right." I press Stop and Rewind. "What's the problem?"

"Well, I've been thinking that I never learned how to sew."

"A lot of girls your age don't know how to sew."

"Does Keara know?"

"Yeah, but she's a lot older and there's a lot I haven't taught her."

"Do *you* know how to sew?"

"Yeah, I know the basics and I have a sewing machine."

"And you made some quilts."

"Yeah."

"Aunt Martha?"

"*Yes,* Jade?"

"Will you teach me?" She wants it so badly.

"Yeah, sweetie. I'll teach you. Okay?" I ask.

"Okay!"

She snuggles back under the quilt and I click on the video. About thirty seconds in, Jade starts tapping my shoulder. "Excuse me, Aunt Martha?"

"Yes, Jade?" I feel my teeth grinding together.

"Can I ask you something?"

I stop the tape.

"*Yessss.*"

"When?"

"When *what*?"

"*When* will you teach me to sew?"

"I don't know."

"Maybe tonight?" she asks.

"No. You came over for dinner and a movie. Plus, I don't have any sewing stuff around."

"When *can* we?"

"I don't know. I'll have to think about it."

"Okay."

"Now, Jade, I'm gonna turn this back on and I expect us to watch it together, quietly. And if you think of questions, be sure to remember them and we'll talk about them after. Okay?"

"Yeah."

We watch the video punctuated every few minutes by questions like, "What's gonna happen next? Why did that happen?" She's so impatient she can't stand to wait till the next scene to know what's going to happen. And we're not talking cliff-hangers here. Anne of Green Gables is about as basic as you can get.

"Jade, just watch and you'll see," I tell her for the tenth time.

It takes a while but she starts getting into it. She loves the feisty Anne. When Matthew, who, with his sister, Marilla, adopted and raised Anne, has a heart attack and dies, Jade becomes totally engrossed. Matthew's funeral is only briefly portrayed, with more emphasis on the people outside the service and their sharing their grief. "This is sad," she says. "Why are they like that?"

"Like what?"

"In those clothes?" She points to the TV.

"Those clothes" refers to the late-nineteenth-century fashions—the women wearing long black dresses and black hats, and the men dressed severely in black suits. "They're in mourning. Black is color of mourning."

"But what is mourning?"

"Mourning is the time after someone you love dies and you let everyone know you're sad by what you wear and what you do or don't do. It's a time for grief."

"What's grief?"

"It's a deep, sad feeling that people get when they've lost someone they really love."

"Oh," she snuggles back under the quilt and is uncharacteristically quiet for a few minutes.

"I have a black skirt. But I don't think I have a black shirt," she says solemnly.

Oh . . . we've crossed over into another place. I feel it in my bones. "Well, people don't *have* to wear black, especially *now*. Remember, this movie is about a *long* time ago."

"Did you wear black when Brian's mom died?"

"Yeah, I guess I did but that's because I wear a lot of black."

"Why?"

"It's sort of fashionable, plus people say it makes you look thinner."

"Oh, I never heard that."

"It doesn't matter, honey. When you mourn someone you love, it doesn't matter what you wear. It's what you feel that's important."

"I think you're right." She cuddles close, all over my personal space. "Let's keep watching, I love this." She's asleep in ten minutes. The little "big girl."

GOING TO SEE MISS RACHEL AND MR. GRAY

*I*t's taken forever to get this particular sleep over at my sister Rachel's off the ground. With six kids, the possibility of nonnegotiable deal breakers is enormous. In addition, Deven's most recent scan this week shows "something." After two years, it's not surprising. It's always "something." But it heightens the alarm about his catching something from the other kids. It seems that each of them has contracted some germy malady the day before previous D days, and to the great dismay of all concerned, these trips had to be canceled.

No one says it out loud, but these days it takes so much less to sound the alarm that cancels the get-together. The simplest of bugs that the other five kids can quickly shake off carries disaster potential for Deven. The outside world has a certain degree of enemy-territory quality to it, and Rachel and Raina are the generals, constantly vigilant about degrees of exposure and levels of readiness for the missions to safely begin. Fever/no fever, spots/no spots, throw up or all clear; then follow lists of excruciating precision: are all looking good; health infractions are minor, temporary, and noncontagious. Just how you like 'em.

Friday morning comes and we are all psyched. Darren has already phoned to tell me what he's packed—noteworthy is the absence of clothes—unless a bathing suit counts. Basketball, baseball, soccer, skates . . . his *bike*.

"Darren, you know how much Sean and the girls have of all that stuff," I say, trying to encourage him to cut back.

"Yeah, but I want my own."

"We can't bring your bike." He's mad, because ever since Tori and Gracie have moved into their new house, he's been transfixed by the boys whizzing by around the cul de sac on their brilliantly painted and accessorized bikes, with helmets to match. I know he's dying to ride with the big boys, but he and Tori can go out and do about all the biking he's prepared for.

"What about your clothes?"

"I'll just wear the same stuff I'm wearing."

"At night?" I ask.

"Aunt Martha," he whispers into the phone, "that's not a problem."

"Of course it is. You have to have something to throw on at night."

"No, I don't. Oh . . . yeah," he says, "but the *other* . . . it's not a problem. You don't have to make a liner for my sleeping bag or Miss Rachel doesn't have to get a pad for a bed."

"Oh, no? Have you stopped being a deep sleeper?" one of our face-saving euphemisms for bed-wetting.

"Well, no, I'm still a deep sleeper, but they make these things now that look like regular underwear and if you wear 'em, you don't wet the bed. And the next day, no one knows."

"That is very interesting. I know a couple of guys, older than you, who would be interested in something like that for themselves. Sometime maybe you could show or tell me where to get it. . . . Boy, don't you wish you thought of inventing it!"

"We'd be a millionaire!" he exclaims.

"Darren, I still think it would be a good idea to bring another pair of shorts and a T-shirt. I mean, now that you're getting older, it's not as easy to exchange clothes with anyone else. I mean, like what if you slide in the mud or run through a sprinkler or something and you're soaked? Seeing you in Barbie shorts and Little Mermaid T-shirt would be pretty interesting."

"Gross. I'm bringin' my own clothes."

"Hey, pal, while I have you on the phone, do me a favor. Will you play with Sean a little? He thinks you're so big and so cool. I know being with a little kid can slow you down, but you'll be surprised at how much bigger he's gotten."

"Okay, but I really need time to hang out with Uncle Brian and Mr. Grey, so let's just see."

Initially, Deven took it as a personal affront to his independence and maturity that Raina was sleeping over, too. But there is complete agreement among the grown-ups that her presence is a necessity that Deven will appreciate only when he can't go to sleep. No one can give him his medicine like his mom, no one can lie down next to him like his mom, and no one can help soothe the pain as well as his mom. It makes more sense to him when Raina explains how much she's missed Rachel and how long she's wanted to see the new house.

Rachel, in my opinion, is in the same major league of great motherhood as Raina. There's something about the two of them—they work their asses off, they love their kids like crazy, and their kids are secure in the knowledge that they are uniquely wonderful. So Deven has little trouble buying the fact that Mom wants to see *her* friends Rachel and Greg.

Darren and Jade can't stand still as we load the van. It is hard to get Deven in "his seat"—the only bucket seat in the minivan, and the kids always fight over it. We settle in his blankets and pillow and construct a makeshift footrest if he needs it. He has sunglasses, which he refuses to wear, a baseball cap in reserve, and a lighter golf cap to help keep the sun out of the eyes. His response to everything is crankiness. He constantly rubs his bad eye and squints and moves with discomfort. He can't get comfortable. Was this a good idea? But he has been looking forward to it all week, insistent that he is fine. Right before we leave, Raina gives him some pain medicine, which should ease the fifty-minute drive for him, perhaps even let him sleep.

By the time we hit the road, it's early evening on a Friday, just a *perfect* time to drive from suburban Virginia to suburban Maryland. Darren commands Brian to use his "shortcuts" and accuses him of holding out when the trip seems too long.

Raina sits up front with Brian and I'm way back on the bench seat with the Jade and Darren, who piss me off in the very first minutes. A fraction of an inch of a butt that threatens to trespass on the space of another is cause for major contention.

When Brian yells for them to settle down, Jade complains that there isn't as much room in the back as usual, smartly avoiding the issue of the size of my fat ass and leaving it as a general problem. Then there is the problem of who sits on the hump the longest. I have made it clear I am never sitting on it, which means that there will have to be an absolutely fair point when the exchange will take place between Darren and Jade.

"But, Uncle Brian," Darren whines, "how will you know *exactly* when I get to move to the window seat?"

"I have the alarm on my phone."

"Yeah, but what if the trip takes longer than usual? Then someone could get the seat longer than someone else."

"I'll tell you what," Brian sighs, "any unequal time on the hump going to Rachel and Greg's, we'll make up coming back."

During the next few seconds I can almost watch the wheels

turn in the mind of this child who was born to be a lawyer. He shifts uncomfortably on the hump and then pronounces, "It's fair, as long as you aren't talking to my mom so much you can't hear the alarm."

"Darren," Brian says with controlled exasperation, "here's the alarm." He presses a button. A fairly obnoxious and loud sound emanates from the front seat, disturbing Deven's rest and impressing the hell out of Darren. "Do you think that's loud enough?" demands Brian.

"Oh, yeah, that's a good one. I won't miss it," Darren promises.

"Darren," Jade criticizes from the window seat, "you are such a baby."

"I am not . . . *Mo-om*, Jade said I was a baby."

I know for a fact that Raina can hear him, but she keeps on talking to Brian and listening to music like they're the only two people in the car. "I'm not kidding you two," I threaten. "If you don't stop this nonsense, we're going home."

"You're not the boss of this car. It's Uncle Brian's van," Darren challenges me.

"Oh? Do you want to see how fast I can get Uncle Brian to turn this car around?" I one-up him.

Silence.

Jade sits still, like a candidate for sainthood.

"That goes for you, too, Miss Jade," I hold out. "*No one* in this car is a baby."

Darren corrects me, " 'Cept for the one in Mommy's tummy."

I laugh. "You're absolutely right. Now let's just have a good ride."

He leans his head against my shoulder in a silent assent and secret pleasure in once again having the last word.

Deven complains that the air-conditioning is too high. We adjust his blankets and turn it down. Darren and Jade register the higher temperature and complain. Even the music is a point of contention. Darren wants Great Big Sea—his loud, pulsing link to Uncle Brian. It's amazing that he knows the rocking melodies and lyrics so well with fairly limited exposure. Brian tells him it's too loud for Deven. So Darren tries to get Deven to say he wants it—which he doesn't. I'm rooting against Darren because I really don't want Raina to hear the drunken, racy songs her son has osmosed as the pearls of our heritage. Brian puts on a classical station, which satisfies no one. He and Raina talk quietly and I feel like one of the cranky little kids in the back.

As we get closer, we pass the familiar landmarks—a series of huge, ornate churches, temples, and mosques. Darren and Jade compete with each other.

"Take a right."

"No, take a left."

Fortunately, Brian has a very good compass in his head. Raina can't believe the size of the houses, and all of a sudden I feel embarrassed by the obvious wealth of the development where three-car garages and houses with long lawns back up to a sprawling golf course. The kids have been here several times before, but Raina remembers only Rachel's previous modest house—quite different from this one.

"Mom," Darren yells from the back. "Wait till you see it. It's like a hotel."

We pull into the driveway and instantly see that there's trouble in paradise. Deven is pretty groggy and willing to wait in his seat while the grown-ups hash it out. Darren and Jade leap out of the car, on the immediate lookout for their favorite things.

Greg, in the midst of a monster hug from Darren says, "Hey pal, stay right here for a second."

Tori, Gracie, and Sean are sitting on the picnic table. Something is up.

Rachel is still in her work suit. "We have a problem."

Gracie runs over with the ugliest doll I have ever seen clutched in her hands. It's more like a troll. A really awful troll. "Can I give it to him?" motioning to Deven.

"Gracie," Rachel says firmly, "go back and sit on the picnic table."

Greg explains that there was a kid playing at the house all day and the parents just called to say that he is puking his guts out. It is only then that the kid's mother, a doctor, told Greg that through the week, they'd all been on IV fluids at home for a few hours after puking and went back to being fine. "I got really pissed and reminded her I had an immune-suppressed kid coming," he tells Raina.

Rachel has a can of Lysol in her hand and says, "We traced his steps, and the kids spent the whole day outside. The only place inside he could have possibly been is the sunroom, which is a relatively small space, almost like a glassed-in porch, where the kids have toys and arts and crafts things. I've Lysoled everywhere. Deven doesn't like this space. He likes the family room."

Rachel leads Raina to the TV room—a large, carpeted, barely furnished room with a comfy leather chair and hassock Deven likes. And a couch already covered with a sheet and pillows. Raina looks around, holding Deven, who clearly wants to stay. Rachel, who would Lysol her own children if she could, finally settles down. The children are given permission to scatter to their favorite places together. Gracie still has that awful doll. She wants to give it to Deven.

I can see Tori solemnly register the changes in Deven since

the last time she saw him, only a couple of months ago. He is clearly more emaciated and the right side of his head and neck is swollen and distorted. Gracie runs in with her wretched doll for Deven. After he is settled on the couch she tries to give it to him again. Tori, feeling the weight of a higher level of understanding of Deven's illness, tries to grab it from Grace, yelling, "You can't give him that beast. It's dirty and germy."

So Gracie takes it to the kitchen, covers it with Lysol, grabs it by its long, multicolored hair, and swings it around to dry it off. Satisfied that she's done all she can, she presents it to him again. He's not at his most alert, but he accepts it from her and motions for her to put it near him, not on him. She is seized by her own goodness.

I'm in the kitchen with Raina and Rachel, catching up with my sister Priscilla, who has just dropped by to see us all. Gracie snuggles on my lap, wraps her arms around my neck, and says, "I gave Deven my doll."

"Oh really, honey?"

"Aren't I generous? Aren't I kind?"

"Oh yes, Gracie, that was a lovely thing to do." She gives me a blissful smile as if she inhabits the state of perfection on a regular basis. This is the child who the week before was so angry at her little brother, Sean, that she screamed, *"I don't love you."* When he didn't respond with the level of distress she expected, she pulled out the big guns. *"Sean, Jesus doesn't even love you!"*

She hops off my lap and goes looking for "the guys." Priscilla takes the moment to not so subtly ask whether it had been my plan to wear my cotton jumper inside out. This cracks everyone at the table up. "Everybody makes a mistake now and then," I defend myself as I run to the nearby bathroom to make the correction.

Raina, Rachel, and Priscilla, amid a great deal of laughter, recount numerous clothing infractions I've committed over the past few years.

"Go ahead. Laugh at my expense," I say, hoping that guilt will shut them up.

Raina leans over and checks that the tag is on the inside and on the back of my jumper. "Good work," she pronounces like I'm a little kid.

Deven has a video on in the background and seems relatively comfortable. I wonder if he can hear his mother's laughing voice and if it doesn't give him peace.

Gracie comes back into the house and asks Brian to walk her across part of the golf course that abuts their new house to find the other kids. "I'm afraid of bats flying in my hair," she tells him.

They walk barefoot across the lush green.

"Brian?" she asks. "Do you know why I wanted to give Deven, the sick boy, my special doll?" Brian, who's been having a hard time lately—getting easily choked up when it comes to Deven—is prepared to be moved.

"No, Gracie, why?"

"Well, first of all," she reflects in her sweet, soft voice, "I didn't really want it anymore. And . . . well . . ." She hesitates, then confides in him. She stops walking and looks him straight in the eye. "I've been having a lot of trouble with ogres lately."

DULCE DOMUM

He saw clearly how plain and simple it all was; — how narrow, even — but clearly, too, how much it all meant to him, and the special value of some such anchorage in one's existence. . . . But it was good to think he had this to come back to, this place which was all his own, these things which were so glad to see him again and could always be counted upon for the same simple welcome.

KENNETH GRAHAME, *The Wind in the Willows*

 t some point in documenting the progress of Raina's house, I was driven to go riffling through the bookcases in Keara's old room. We almost wore out the book *The Wind in the Willows* as we followed the adventures of Mr. Toad, Mole, Badger, and Rat. Lately, I keep going back for the more mystical descriptions of the quest not only for the physical place but also for the emotional contentment that is "home."

Despite fears that the eight town houses would never be ready on time, by some miracle, they are—almost. Moving in will take another week or two. The day of the dedication ceremony was spring in Virginia at its very best—crisp and sunny, with the abounding of new growth. When we arrive we're given a booklet with a wonderful Habitat graphic on the cover. The biggest word is "Dedication"—a great word to describe the ritual of blessing of houses as well as what it took to turn a barren piece of land on the corner of Kenmore and Glebe into a residential neighborhood—owned by the people who did it themselves with a whole lot of help—Eli, Paul, Nikki, Raina, and friends. The quote on the cover is one that no one could find objection to: "Bless these homes and the families who will live in them."

The partner families, Habitat volunteers, and staff spill over from the sidewalk into the street in front of the yellow and white town houses. Everyone is settling down for the actual program, but it is almost redundant. Joy abounds.

The president of the local Habitat chapter opens the service. An Arlington county councilwoman makes introductory remarks. There are several invocations by local clergy. The Messiah Methodist Church Choir hits the nail on the head with the hymn "Plenty Good Room." Then each family is called up and given two things: the precious keys to their new house, and, since all eight families are Christian, a Bible. Raina's Habitat sponsor arranged for the twins to memorize a short presentation of the keys.

The boys are serious in their "church clothes." Deven's weight loss is so dramatic that his belt deserves a special award for holding up his pants. He's been saddled with another nickname by his cousin CeCe: No Tush. His hair is growing in again, resembling the early strands of grass on his new front lawn. The boys have trouble with their timing, so it's hard to understand them, but they are very sincere. Raina holds them both to her as she takes her keys, and they emerge from the hug with shining smiles.

Jade looks like one of the Disney princesses of her dreams. Her hair is pulled straight back and styled in a bun just like the one their mother wears. She shimmers in the sunlight in a pink chiffon dress, white tights, and patent leather shoes. She proudly hands her mother a brand-new Bible.

Elizabeth, who put in a lot of sweat equity, is beaming. Raina's sister Alana and her fiancé, Robert; Alana's daughter,

CeCe; Kendra and her daughter, Jah Nel; Raina's brother Terrence and his year-old twins, Samuel and David; and Howard are there. My parents, Rachel, Greg, Tori, Gracie, and Sean are there. Brian and I are there with bells on.

We end with a benediction over the families and their new homes: "Blest be the tie that binds"

> Blest be the tie that binds
> Our hearts with Christian love;
> The fellowship of kindred minds
> Is like to that above.

After refreshments, Raina's and my family retreat to my house, only about a mile away, for a celebration potluck dinner. When Raina actually moves in, Elizabeth and I are planning to throw her a housewarming shower. But we wanted to do something on the day of dedication. Brian got a cooked and carved ham and rolls, and we all made dishes to go around it. I made an adult cake and then we bought a lot of those really gross cupcakes with multicolored frosting made with 95 percent shortening and cake that is half air. Children love them.

The kids disappear with each other to different corners of the house and backyard. My parents give Raina housewarming gifts—cards from my sisters and brothers with money for the down payment and a painting by my mother. Brian and I give her some practical gifts, some sentimental gifts, and some just plain silly, stupid joke gifts. Rachel and Greg give her chairs that Raina had already picked out. But then they carry in something I know she's really wanted. It's all wrapped up, and she calls the kids to help unwrap (rip the hell out of it). They do their job with relish, and in short order it becomes clear that it's a bunk bed and two mattresses for Jade's room. Raina goes from a huge smile, then puts her head down and starts to cry. Really hard. Rachel gets down next to Raina on the floor and puts her arms around her. I can see that Rachel is crying, too.

Everyone remains silent. No one rushes in to get things back on track. There are so many reasons to cry—in joy and in sorrow. And they mix together like the embrace of Rachel and Raina.

Raina wipes her eyes and says, "I am so blessed."

As Brian gives her a hand up off the floor he quips, "Boy, I'm glad we didn't get you that hot tub," which makes everyone laugh.

Darren and Deven get pillows and "kid pillowcases" with characters they love. Jade gets girly-girl sheets and some neat matching storage boxes for her room. After dinner, the kids, who've been unusually quiet, request our presence in the backyard. With brooms, rakes, dustpans, bats, and other creative tools, they have totally swept the brick patio of the thick blanket of leaves that remained there all winter. They are absolutely thrilled at their success. Of course, no one has a camera. Brian and Greg have the kids line up and have them describe their specific task before they dispense one dollar to each child. It is so funny, made even happier when my dad says, "Next year, Raina, all these workers will be in *your* yard."

BIG BROTHER AND DAN RATHER

*I*t's Friday. I'm at the oncologist's office. Raina has a doctor's appointment of her own, so here I am in Room 7 of the Fairfax Oncology Group with Deven, who is getting some badly needed platelets. Tuesday's didn't hold him. When Raina picked him up from her sister Alana's, after a few hours on Thursday, Deven's face was streaked with blood. This is the quickest blood flow I've seen. Getting platelets will at least slow it down.

Deven lies on a low blue-canvas cot with his bloodied *Sesame Street* pillow that I had made but now need to dismantle, wash, and then sew back together. At least three children are crying in different rooms. There's the shrill protests of a baby, the angry resistance of a toddler, and the agony of an eight-year-old. Somewhere behind those noises I hear the improbable but necessary laughter of the staff, the voice of Dr. Silverstein telling grateful parents in the next room that he is "reassured" by something. That precious word, not one I've heard connected to Deven in a long time.

I am weary. Not tired, exactly. There's a difference. Sleep cures tired.

I'm blunted, irritable, put out. Last night I had a fit because President George W. Bush had the nerve to preempt the show *Big Brother*—which has to be one of the lowest forms of video entertainment in existence. I was initially embarrassed to admit it to anyone but Brian, who shamefully watches it, too. Then I slipped to Raina, who confessed that whenever possible she watches. The president is talking about abortion and stem cell research—an issue that is actually highly relevant to our lives over the past few years—but all I wanted was to watch seven people lie, backstab, seduce, and cheat their way to a possible $500,000 grand prize. (Whenever the people talk to each other, they say things like "I love you to death," which is never a good sign for the recipient, because it means he is going to be screwed over in the not so distant future.)

Kent, the older guy (translation: my age) who got kicked out last night, started to mouth off—moralizing about all the

"freaks" in the house. There was something in his holier-than-
thou farewell—"I can look my children in the face, the way I
played this game. . . ." —like somehow he played the game with
one ounce more nobility than anyone else, that made me wish
that just for whining, they'd take away the car he'd won. I am so
goddamn sick of whining—Jade's, Darren's, Kent's . . . mine.

However, all was not lost. After Bush's half-assed and totally confusing stem cell announcement, Dan Rather came back
on. I expected one of those typically tiresome post-speech analy-
ses. Political pundits usually spend more time explaining the
speech—for those of us idiots who can't possibly understand it
than the speech itself actually lasts. But maybe Dan Rather
was weary, too, basically announcing that President Bush said
x, y, and z, repeating the main points. But then Rather took a
wonderful detour: "It's a very complicated issue that TV really
can't do justice to, so read about it tomorrow in your paper.
Good night."

I loved it! It made me so stupidly happy. A respected jour-
nalist just looks you straight in the eye and says, *This is so
complicated.*

At my most suspicious, I wonder if the network's financial
considerations engineered the seeming humility. The "numbers" probably indicate that people would prefer to watch the
conniving, one-upsmanship on *Big Brother* rather than a cadre
of pundits and researchers bullshitting on something labeled
the "news." Let's face it, the really important stuff *never* fits between commercials.

THE SPLIT

*D*even hates my guts. In my head, I know that he still loves me, but right now it's a love that seethes and bites and screams. In the shrink business we call this "splitting." In a relationship, you can go from all good to all bad. For as much as you were once close to perfect, you are now a complete fuck-up. For as much as you were once breathtakingly beautiful, you are now a hag, as bad as the worst Disney witch. Where you were once kind and generous, you are now stingy and vicious. For as much as you were once so sweetly loved, you are now relentlessly despised.

This change has evolved over the past few weeks. Deven's split is between me and Raina. He needs his mother so constantly, so totally that he can't afford to unload all his anger and fear and pain at the risk of alienating her. So he chooses a stand-in, a substitute mom, to whom he was very close, and puts all the awfulness on her. Unfortunately "bad mom" is me.

All the psychological insight in the world is of absolutely no comfort to me now. It hurts. Even in the smallest moments, I am at fault. Deven sits on Raina's lap at my dining-room table, providing a litany of my faults. "And you wouldn't let me go to McDonald's." He points at me accusingly, so angry his little finger shakes.

Raina laughs and gives him a hug. "Deven, that wasn't Aunt Martha. *I* was the one who wouldn't let you go."

"No, no," he objects. "It was *her.*"

"No, sweetie," Raina insists gently. "Remember Aunt Martha was all ready to take you and I said no?"

"*No!* It was Aunt Martha." He slams his fist on the table. "She is so mean. I remember. You didn't do it. She *did!*"

Raina shrugs.

He folds his arms across his chest in a world-class pout.

I go to the kitchen to wash the dishes and nurse my wounds.

THE SONOGRAM

*R*aina dropped Deven and me off at his doctor's so that he wouldn't be alone while she drove a couple of miles away for her first sonogram. Deven is ignoring me, communicating his disdain so well with a look, a shrug, a dismissing wave of his hand. He's getting blood, platelets, and some chemo.

Sally, one of Deven's most prized nurses, taps on the door and whispers to me to pick up the blinking line on the phone next to me. Deven, who's been pretending to be asleep, opens one eye to see if there's anything of interest to him.

I pick up the phone, and on the other end is a voice I barely recognize.

"It's a boy!" Raina crows. "December seventeenth," she almost sings. Her voice is giggly, light, and happy. I haven't heard her like that in months. "The technician pointed out different views—the arms, the hands. He said, 'It looks like he's praying.' Can you believe that?"

"Did you get a good look at the jewels?" I'm trying to be discreet with Deven listening in.

"The jewels?" Raina repeats.

"The *family* jewels . . . ," I say a little more. "The Johnson."

She laughs loudly and says, "Martha, I swear sometimes. Girl, you are a mess. But, yeah, we got a couple of good shots."

"And how sure are we that there's only *one* in there?"

"They are almost certain there is only one in there."

"And everything is okay with you and the baby?"

"Praise the Lord, everything is fine."

It is so strange for her to be across Route 50 with her new son while I am here at another doctor's with Deven. He is stretched across a green lounge chair, his poor little bald head resting on the puffy arm. He's dressed as his usual dapper self—patent leather shoes, black socks on his matchstick ankles, gray flannel dress pants, and a bright blue dress shirt tucked in at his tiny waist. The right side of his face is swollen. On the trip back from Rachel and Greg's last week we knew something was going wrong when he plaintively yelled to Raina, "Mama, Mama, I can't see." He's partially lost sight in his right eye, which has deep bruised half-moons under it. To look at him straight on is to register the aggressive and relentless march of this cancer. But at the moment he is in left profile and is as beautiful a boy as he ever was—long dark eyelashes, cupid lips although more gray now than red. His little chest works so hard as he sleeps. But he is peaceful, a state he so deserves but experiences so rarely. His fingers are delicate; his hands are the size of a child at least two years younger. A little old man.

For almost the whole time I have known him, I have had unlimited two-way communication with him. Now he refuses to let me near him. He says he hates the sound of my voice. He blames me, listing my transgressions, some of which are quite old.

It hurts to know that this child—who could instantly and magically find a comfortable place on my hip, lap, back, or arms—now considers them toxic. So I search for ways of giving him vicarious comfort—sewing him a pink flannel half-moon pillow that he can rest his head more gently against the old mainstay of Brian's study—now Deven's own recliner in their house.

I suddenly think of the pink rocker and matching hassock that he could sit in and rock with me for hours. Even though we both agreed from the outset that his mother had a much, much, much better voice than mine, he'd accept my songs if I'd sing softly. We fit into each other in that unique way that children of certain ages and mothers of certain sizes can mold together in an incredibly satisfying connection. Then, as he got older, I got more directions on how to sing, how to rock, criticisms about the liberties not so easily taken anymore.

"Hey, why are you always kissin' me on my head?" He'd swipe my hand away.

"Because it's always here," and I'd sneak a kiss. Once he'd lost his hair, he made it clear he didn't want kisses anymore, but he became fascinated by the ways our hands fit together, how many of his fingers would fit around mine. We would rock and sing, or not. And talk, or not.

Will he ever let me hold him again?

A SECRET LIFE

*W*illiam has evaporated. Raina began to notice things that she couldn't explain. Despite his accompanying her to church, despite his stated plans to join her church, it never seemed to happen. He stopped working at Harris Teeter, the grocery store where they'd met. Apparently, he has another life. Over time Raina has learned that. He lives with a woman and her son and has no plans to change. He's been able to pull the deception off so long because the woman works nights. There were so many lies—about a future that now doesn't include Raina, her children . . . *or* his own new son. It doesn't

make sense. He really seemed like such a good guy. I thought
he was going to make a good father . . . and I really hoped that
maybe there was "something there" in terms of a future with
Raina. I am incredulous that some guy would do this to my
friend. And how we could all be so fooled. I wonder if he will
be a father to the new baby. I have a very bad feeling that he
won't, that he's just gone. Raina is mystified and devastated. I'd
like to hunt him down and slug him.

OBITUARY FOR A LITTLE GIRL

*R*eading my morning *Washington Post*, I'm stopped short
by a picture of a little girl, Deven's age, who died of
cancer. With her braids and the gaps in her smile awaiting the
big-girl teeth, she was adorable. I check, and I'm in the "Death
Notices" section. An obituary of a child in the newspaper? The
long column was obviously written by her family—so unlike
the obituaries of adults. We know her favorite color and what
she liked to do with her little brother. Then it hit me. It said so
much more than the facts of the life of this particular girl. It
said something about *all* children—that their lives are full, that
their accomplishments are many.

I don't romanticize children, nor do I think of them as
miniature adults. But every child is a full person at her particular point in time. And it doesn't matter that he hasn't held some
government job for thirty-seven years or she hasn't patented
some gadget or graduated from grade school, for that matter.

This little girl *lived*. She learned. She had strong likes and
dislikes. She came to know the world in her own way. Right up
until the end of her illness she took on her days with an energy

and abandon most grown-ups envy. In her six years she had clearly already let love in and was wonderful at spreading it around.

Her little picture in the paper underestimates her large but brief life. But just as she deserved to live her life fully till the very end, she now deserves to have it recognized fully, whether she's six or sixty.

FAITH

I feel tension with Raina about faith and how it relates to illness and death, healing and hospice. She hates the idea of hospice. While acknowledging that their services are something she needs, accepting those services is, to her, an admission of some kind of defeat—an expression of the limits of belief in a healing God. I don't see it that way. I just don't. Maybe I'm too pragmatic. I want their services. I don't care about the vocabulary of it. I asked her to just set up an appointment for an introductory interview, no strings attached.

It would be good to find out what services hospice provides and whether they might be consistent with her faith. Hospice is by definition an organization that assists people with dying— offering a number of different ways to help, either at home or at a hospice center so a person doesn't have to die in a hospital. The inherent problem is, of course, that you have to accept the dying part. To some people this means giving up on the possibility of healing at whatever time God chooses, and that makes it difficult to reconcile.

I suggest that maybe it's the kind of thing she should talk to her pastor about. Not just because he's her pastor, but because

he recently lost his daughter to breast cancer. Without missing
a beat, she exclaims, "He would *never* have used hospice."

Okay. There it is. The bar, the standard she has set for herself. *She* has to take care of it all herself. *She* has to keep the
faith—by not admitting that taking help from hospice means
submitting to words like "terminal," like dying. It's like admitting that God has thrown up His hands and Raina's impas-
sioned prayers are nullified. I am so torn between wanting her
to do it *my* way. Be pragmatic. Accept any help hospice can offer. Swallow the stuff you don't like. I feel that bossy, pushy,
big sister popping out—the one who knows exactly how things
should be done. I can be utterly disorganized in my own life,
but I'm always quite happy to offer or inflict my services on the
lives of others. My pragmatic approach to hospice is, "Oh, screw
it. It's free. It doesn't mean you have to believe anything."

But to Raina this is a door she does not want to open. And
no one hired me to open it. I keep wanting to find things to *do*.
And yet if I think about the Scripture that both Raina and I
were raised on, in his final hours Jesus asked His dearest
friends to *be* with Him. And truly being with Him in His agony,
in the contemplation of what was to be His fate, was the hard-
est thing they could do.

I know the feeling.

HOSPICE—STRIKE ONE

I'm afraid the hospice intake people aren't listening closely
enough to Raina, to her belief in the possibility that Deven
might be healed, even in the midst of his dying. Some would
call her stance denial; perhaps part of it is. But the sincerity of

her faith must be honored. What *she* heard was *Deven is dying. All hope for recovery is nil. We want to help you with his death.*

Raina needs people who can observe honestly that her son is fading, but work with her within her own faith, to acknowledge that Deven may not be healed within her definition but in God's. But to do that right now feels unfaithful. The best way to use them is not for their counseling and emotional support, which I've seen as so helpful to some families. Raina can get her support elsewhere. What she needs is the nursing support services they provide so that Deven can be at home if possible and avoid the hospital and perhaps some of the arduous visits to the doctors' office.

WWJD (WHAT WOULD JESUS DO?)

*W*hen Raina and I began our friendship I always assumed the race difference would be the biggest challenge to overcome, managing those assumptions, hurts, and distrusts that seem to exist on a cellular level between blacks and whites. There are trip wires to mines so deeply embedded in the landscape. A million "You go, girlfriends" or "You're da' man" or high fives inevitably fail to protect us from that deeper knowledge of ourselves and each other. The wounds of race in this country are pervasive and not easily healed.

But my whiteness and her blackness are a fact of our friendship. We've gotten to know each other's individual experiences, attitudes, and the unconscious culture carried within. As we bang up against the differences in real-life moments, we are confronted by the fact that often we don't know what we don't know. But there is a safe comfort between us—I don't

know why—that allows her to say what she thinks, allows me
to ask questions that reveal my total ignorance.

Raina's niece CeCe, a very talented young woman who is
an incredible mimic, does a white woman (with a pole up her
ass) imitation at a big family cookout where we are the only
white people. There is no hurt intended, conveyed, or received.
She's just very funny. At that same picnic, someone asks Jade
who the white people are, pointing to us. Jade replies, "There's
no white people here." The person points to us and says,
"Yes, there are. Them." Jade shrugs, and replies, "That's just
Uncle Brian and Aunt Martha. They don't count." Whatever
that means.

When the boys were babies, I remember Raina complaining about how long their hair was getting. After a couple of
times, I said what I thought was the obvious, "Well why don't
you go ahead and get it cut?" We were in a room full of black
women, who all turned and looked at me like I was from Sat-
urn. "You don't cut a black boy's hair before his first birthday,"
one woman told me like it was the eleventh Commandment.

"Oh," I said meekly.

Two years later, I felt comfortable enough to ask, "Why
not?" And, after they explained that it's so the texture of the
child's hair is not ruined, I was okay challenging, "Is that really
true, or is it an old wives tale?" And we talked about it. It's
a process. Sometimes confusing. Sometimes funny. Sometimes
bumpy.

But the biggest difference between us—two Christian
women—is our faith. At the bottom of it is that Raina's faith
is solid and mine constantly wavers. The other issue is that
our Christian faiths are so different. It probably sounds naive
to scholars of religions, but it confounds me that Christ, this
one man, could spawn so many religions that believers see as

simultaneously consistent and inconsistent with the Scripture left behind. The Catholic approach was to elaborate — adding a whole lot to the original. The more ritual and rules, the better. I was raised in the late fifties and sixties, memorizing the Baltimore Catechism of the Catholic Church; Raina was raised on Bible passages.

Frankly, in my growing up, Scripture took a backseat to the knowledge of Catholicism. We learned the stories, but in a different way than Raina. I am the product of twelve years of Catholic school and I'm always blown away when someone says "James, verses five through twelve" and can quote them word for word. And yet give me a fountain pen and one of those blue examination books and I can write the answer to "What is the Mass?" — a kicker question from the catechism, very long and involved — and not get a preposition or a punctuation mark out of place. We got our Scripture at Mass during the gospels and the sermons I almost never understood.

Raina's faith and my faith have been a source of conversation, an inquiry in which I often just write myself off as a lapsed Catholic heathen and her as dedicated to her nondenominational evangelical Christian church. Her congregation is very expressive in church, and even speaks in "the gift of tongues." The thought of people raising their hands in the air, yelling "Amen," while a Catholic priest is preaching is hair-raising. In most Catholic churches, it would be a major freak-out. Raina's religion is a strict faith: no drinking, no trick-or-treating. They emphasize the presence of evil, the devil. More fire and brimstone than I'm used to. Which is strange because in Catholicism you can practically go to Hell for sneezing the wrong way. We all get to Hell by different routes. God only knows how we all get to Heaven.

Raina's faith is the center of her existence and an important

bond among the people in her family. I am so angry at the
Catholic Church for its position on women and all the related
rules that don't make sense to my life. I still practice in other
ways, like saying the rosary and other prayers, like reading the
words of the ancient and more-modern saints or near-saints I
admire.

There are some childhood practices, like saying grace before meals, that I'm sorry I've let go. I was reminded of this the
first time Raina and the kids and I went to McDonald's. Before
a tiny hand touched a Happy Meal, Raina and the children had
hands folded, heads bowed, saying their prayer. I had a bite of
Big Mac in my mouth before I noticed, then quickly bowed my
head while trying to discreetly chew the food already stuffed in
my mouth.

I remember the first time I noticed that our crosses were
different: the ones we wore around our necks, the key chain,
the bumper sticker on her car. Christ was missing from all
of her things. In Catholic objects, Christ is depicted with his
nearly naked, battered body, arms and legs nailed to the cross,
a crown of thorns on his head. Our focus is on the suffering of
Christ on the cross. In Raina's church, it is on the risen Christ.

I have made some changes. I've stopped saying my routine
"Jesus Christ!" as an expression of surprise. I remind the kids
to say their prayers. When I tell them stories from the Bible or
about the saints, I try to put them in generic ways. We bump
along to accommodate each other and respect each other's be-
liefs and practices.

But it's now—now that we're looking at issues of sickness
and healing, living and dying, and, above all, God's will, that
there is a subtle but painful parting of the ways. Raina has
turned down another stem cell transplant—a decision with
which I agree. The chemotherapy is only to hold him, not cure

him. Raina prays by herself, with her family, and her church for a miracle. Her faith in a God who can just reach down and free Deven from the neuroblastoma is so strong. I, too, believe in miracles. But in the meantime my faith tells me that you look at what God's intentions seem to be and work from there.

Deven is losing ground. He is dying. But to say aloud that he is dying feels like blasphemy in Raina's house. She sees it as turning away from the enormous possibilities of prayer, of God's active presence in response. The hard thing is that I want a miracle, but Deven is living and dying at the same time. And in that living, someone's got to talk to him about dying. The psychologist in me feels like the kids need to be talked to: They are confused, hyper, angry. Talking about the possibility of Deven's dying is not going to make him die. Fortunately, Raina has softened to accepting the idea of some of the nursing services hospice can provide.

At this point I'm *praying* that the will of God is to keep Deven alive and make him healthy, but I'm *thinking* that the will of God is going to be something much different. I need to pray for the courage to deal with whatever is in store. Raina and I both believe that whether Deven lives or dies, he will be healed. At least there's that.

The other day, when I came over, CeCe was there. I brought Deven a new video. He was groggy from his meds. CeCe said, half kidding, half seriously, "Aunt Martha spoils you rotten. You are just too spoiled."

Something in me snapped. I said softly in a voice too close to his ear, "I don't know how much longer I have to be with him, so I'm gonna spoil him all I want." I knew I had said the wrong thing. It came out of my anger—not at CeCe or at Raina but at the whole lousy situation.

The next day Raina tells me that CeCe asked her if I have a

problem with my faith. I describe the incident to her. I feel so
defensive. "I just don't get how everyone can walk around like
Deven isn't a critically ill little boy. It just frustrates me. I'm
sorry," I tell her. She's understanding, but I know she thinks I
was wrong. Maybe I was. I can't see my way through this.

And now it's coming up with hospice. Unfortunately, they
sort of bill themselves as working with "terminal" patients and
their families. To accept Deven as terminal means her having to
sacrifice her belief. I don't know what to do. Raina could really
use their help. But it is up to her, not me. I am so confused. So,
probably to her surprise, I pray.

Too Far, too Long

*K*eara has left for Sweden for at least a year. In the five
days leading up to her departure, tensions were high.
The rush to find all the right documentation, refill the medicines, anticipate what she can't get in Sweden, prepare for the
frigid winter and the temperate spring, so Brian's and my infinite questions, plus her own anxiety, led to a number of flare-
ups. Sometimes I think the friction is supposed to be there. It
provides a temporary buffer that helps you feel not so heart-
broken about the separation. But when all the bags were packed,
every detail addressed, we could all take a deep breath. Her
cheeks were flushed with excitement, and Brian and I were
close to tears. As she lined up to board the aircraft, she turned
that one last time to wave good-bye, and I was damned if she
was going to see me cry. I blew her a kiss. Brian yelled for her
to call us—on her layover and when she arrived. Despite her
excited smile I think her eyes were glistening with something

different from pleasure. I had thought all the hard work of parenthood was behind us. But to send your child off to places far
away, places you can't even picture in your mind, God, it's hard.

FIGHTING FOR HIS LIFE

*R*aina has to take Darren to the doctor for a sore throat.
Yesterday, when I was over at their place, Deven was
in his recliner watching a movie, Darren and Jade playing
around him. He wasn't speaking to me, but he seemed to have a
bit more energy and less pain.

Darren yelled to his mother, "Mom, I think I gotta go to my
doctors, 'cuz my throat hurts worse. Maybe I have stressed
throat."

In a know-it-all big-sister voice and pose that I remember
from my own childhood, Jade dismisses his diagnosis. "Oh,
Darren, you just have a bad cold, like what Deven gets."

This is just too much for Deven, who sits straight up in his
chair and yells, "Jade! Darren has a bad cold. I got *cancer!*"

Raina tells me that early this morning she announced to
Deven that Aunt Martha was going to be with him at his doctor's while Darren was at his doctor's. Alarmed he asked, "Is
she gonna drive?"

Raina nodded, and Deven burst out crying—real tears, not
the whiny, tantrum kind. Raina asked what the problem was
with my driving. He cried out, "She gives me a headache!" and
then imitated what would have to be called an old-lady style of
driving, with a good deal of bumpy alternation between the gas
and the brake. Raina told me that Deven imitated my driving
as being jerky and making his head go back and forth. She
tried to tell him that my driving was fine, but then Darren and

Jade both jumped in and started imitating me, too. "Once Deven stopped crying, it really was pretty funny." Raina laughs. "What do you mean 'pretty funny'? What's wrong with my driving?"

"Well, you know how you are . . ."

"Not really . . ."

"Well, I'll show you." She imitated Deven's imitation.

"Gee, thanks . . . but I'm gonna need a second opinion."

Raina bursts out laughing, like she's reliving something hilarious, and answers, "Oh, I don't think we'll have any trouble with that."

When we arrive at Deven's doctor's, Raina and Darren have to leave immediately, because Darren, with his germs, can't be around kids who are immune suppressed from their chemotherapy. I arrive at the same time. The exchange with Deven goes horribly. His favorite nurses finally get him settled in a recliner, getting IV fluids, as well as blood and platelets. All chemotherapy has stopped. There will be no more transplants. His care is palliative. For now it holds him, although the pain is getting worse.

I sit facing him, minding my own business, writing in my journal.

He refuses to even look at me. The extra hydration of the IV fluids takes him by surprise. He screams, *"I have to pee!"*

"Bathroom or cup?" I ask urgently.

"Cuuuuuup! Hurry!"

I run to the next empty exam room and grab some plastic cups. In those few seconds, Deven has lost control of his bladder and peed all over himself.

He is enraged. "You made me pee on myself!" he yells at me. He is standing up, wobbly, connected to wires. In jumping up, somehow his pants and underpants are either halfway up or halfway down, and nothing he does seems to change their status. "You made me!" he rants and cries in his pee-soaked navy shorts and his *Blues Clues* underpants that somehow are going to have to come off over his prize-winning Nike shoes and socks.

He is so enraged that the bloody plug from his routinely bloody nose flies out. Blood shoots from his nose and collects in his mouth. The screaming continues.

"Deven, listen, I know how much you hate being wet. Mommy packed dry clothes."

I get closer to him and display the clothes. "Deven if we stand still, I will help you get more comfortable," I insist.

He starts wildly swinging his arms, aiming at anything in his way. I get too close. Somehow we get physically engaged. In his swinging and swatting, we both get caught up in lines from the IV pole, and every move by either of us makes it worse.

He attacks me with his fingernails and tries to draw me closer so he can finish the job with his teeth. This is like his two-year-old tantrums, but now I can't get out of the way. He is throwing anything he can get his hands on. My face is bleeding. He lurches forward to smash the VCR, pulling some of the wires from their ports.

A nurse comes in with clean clothes he rejects.

"I want my mom!" He cries and screams.

While I reach over to see if I can grab my cell phone and call her, he punches me square in the mouth.

Sally, who is a perfect bet to calm him down, comes in, drawn by the noise. Even *she* doesn't have her immediate magic. "Deven," she tells him firmly, "there is no way I can help you if you don't settle down." With that, she leaves the room.

Deven stands there hiccuping tears, his fists balled. He catches a glimpse of himself in the blank screen of the TV. Blood- and tearstained face and shirt, wet pants around his ankles. This siege is one of many lately, and it's finally done me in. Against my will, I start to cry. Not little polite tears. Real crying.

Sally arrives with Betadine and a bunch of swabs for my scratched face and arms. Deven stands still as he watches her minister to my wounded skin and self.

I wonder if I'll have a black eye.

"Raina just can't leave him with anyone else at the appointments anymore," says Sally.

"Yeah," I say through my tears, "but she has so much going on, how can she not?"

"He may need to be in the hospital." After she bandages me up, she says firmly, "Deven, I'm taking Aunt Martha out to wash the blood off her hand. You can see us through the window in the door."

He says nothing.

Once we're outside, she says, "I think he is going to have to go into the hospital. The platelets aren't holding him and we have to figure out why."

In the room I see a little soldier standing his ground. *Sweet boy, remember me?* I want to say. *Remember when we were on the same side in this war?*

"Raina has got to realize how desperate this situation is," Sally whispers.

"What do you mean?" I ask.

"She has to realize he's dying."

"No . . . she doesn't. At least, she's not ready yet. . . . And she struggles with the healing power of prayer to cure him. And I don't think you can take that away from her . . . not that you'd be able to. Her faith is so strong." To Sally, I can express my frustration at not being able to say aloud that Deven's dying. It's as if Raina and I exist in two very different realities on this issue.

I'm embarrassed that I'm crying, but then I think, *Screw it.*
I'm in an office for children with cancer. If I can't cry here, where can I?
Somehow, with Raina gone, crying feels absolutely in context.
Usually I feel that my crying is a reflection of a hole in the faith
that's keeping everyone else afloat.

We both return to the room. Sally silently changes Deven's
clothes and I collapse into the armchair to survey the damage.

Raina cannot return too soon.

IT'S MY BIRTHDAY AND I'LL CRY IF I WANT TO

*B*rian and I drop by Raina's house for a visit. On the Disney Channel, Mary-Kate and Ashley Olsen are having
one of their innumerable video adventures, and all three children are caught up in it. Raina greets us with big hugs. Darren
and Jade jump up and divert enough attention from the show
to confer kisses before getting back to the Olsen twins.

The house smells like a hospital.

Deven is settled in Brian's old recliner with his *Sesame
Street* pillow and blanket. His right eye is more swollen than
yesterday and his neck is looking worse. Still, he's fairly alert.
Deven smiles at Uncle Brian. And then he makes a big show of
not looking at me.

"Deven, look who's here," calls Raina from the kitchen.

He harrumphs and twists his body toward the wall.

I can't stand this. He is going to die with things like this between us.
Raina is finishing up the dishes.

I sit on the floor close to Deven's chair, but not too close.

Raina yells out, "Someone's birthday is coming soon. . . ."

Darren gets excited. "I know! Aunt Martha's!"

Jade pulls herself away from the TV. "What day is your birthday?" Then, before she gets an answer, she turns to Brian. "What are we gonna do for her birthday?"

"We'll figure something out." He winks at her and Darren like they share a big secret.

I mutter half to myself, half within Deven's earshot, "I don't want to have my birthday this year."

In spite of itself, from behind me a little voice whispers, "Why?"

I stay where I am and I don't look back.

" 'Cuz you're old?" he offers.

"No. You know how sometimes when things have been really hard, you don't want to do fun stuff?"

He's quiet for a few seconds. "Yeah," he answers softly.

Silence sets in between us. I figure our communication is finished, but then his little voice pipes up again. "But you *have* to have your birthday."

"Why?"

" 'Cuz it's what you do—every birthday."

"So you think I should have it?"

"Yeah," he says in a voice that's grown stronger.

"Okay," I say, as if I'm giving in a bit unwillingly. "If you think it's important for me to have my birthday, I'll go along with what you think."

"Yeah, yeah." He nods. "You should."

"Well I don't want any big deal. . . . Where should I have it?"

A little pause. "Here?" he offers.

"At your house? Do you think that would be okay with everyone?"

"Yeah."

"Well, what should I have?"

He thinks about it. "Cake . . . juice packs . . . presents . . .

prizes . . ." He's breathing hard just to keep this level of conversation going.

"What kind of cake?" I ask.

"Ice cream cake," he says with absolute conviction.

"Do you think you can eat ice cream cake?"

"Yeah," he answers confidently, "if it's vanilla and chocolate."

"Okay," I say, as if I am giving in a bit unwillingly. "Well,
maybe."

"You should."

We fall back into the video. I pretend to watch the movie
like it's the most compelling thing I've ever seen on a screen.
He seems to withdraw into his own world.

Two minutes later, I feel his tiny hand on my upper arm.
For the past weeks the only way I've felt that hand is scratching, slapping, pushing, or slamming me. Now it is feather light
as he strokes my arm to get my attention.

"Aunt Martha," he whispers, soft and hoarse, "candles."

"What?"

He tries to lean closer to me, so I decide it's all right to lean
into him.

"Candles," he repeats. Since he was a tiny boy he has loved
candles at our dinner table. Even when the meal was more in
the direction of Burger King than Martha Stewart, he and
Darren have always been quick to find candlesticks, candles,
and matches and a grown-up for the lighting. It blessed each
meal with a certain ritual and magic they adored.

"Yeah, but I wonder who we could get to put the candles
on the cake?" I say, pretending to be honestly distressed.

"Me," he whispers.

"What?" I ask, like I didn't hear. I turn to face him.

"You got me." He looks at me tentatively, like he knows his
answer means much more than volunteering for the job of candle placer. It says *maybe we can be close again.*

My instinct, which fortunately I know is totally inappropriate, is to embrace him tightly and cry, *Oh, of course, baby, oh my God, sweetie, you can light candles forever, you can open my presents, hell . . . you can keep my presents.* . . .

Instead, I try to say casually, "Yeah, as I remember, you are an excellent cake decorator. I'd like for you to do it. Thanks." Then I turn and pretend to watch television, fighting the tears. The video keeps going with the resilient Olsen twins prevailing over one adversity or another. Forty-five seconds later, there's another tap on my arm.

"Aunt Martha?"

Since he calls me by name I turn and look him right in the eye. He returns my gaze. "Yeah, sweetie?"

"What if I can't remember?" he asks plaintively.

Oh God, he knows. It's his fading memory, which he has previously refused to acknowledge. At the prospect of missing something so important, he is now publicly admitting it.

"Deven, I'll remember, and just to be safe I'll tell Mommy and Uncle Brian, and between the four of us, I am positive that one person will remember my birthday and your special plan about it. How does that sound?"

"It's okay." A couple of minutes pass. Another tap on the arm. "Aunt Martha, *when* will you tell Mommy?"

"Oh, I don't know. . . . I'll tell her later. . . ."

Several seconds go by. "Tell her *now.*"

I call Raina into the living room. I tell her in front of him about his idea for my birthday. She can't conceal her pleasure and relief over the change in our relationship. In front of him I tell her that if Deven and I don't remember, we are asking Uncle Brian and her to remind us. Raina assures him she'll remember. Jade and Darren overhear the candle lighting deal and launch into the typical "it's not fair" litany, that, if I'm not mistaken, brings the slightest smile to Deven, who has always loved being the winner in this particular dispute. I offer other things they can do—cut the cake, give out the party bags—none of which is good enough, but they settle back down to the Olsen twins pretty quickly.

Deven turns a bit on his side and lays his hand on my arm, a silent bridge that allows us to remain connected, to travel back and forth. I know it must be taking so much energy to extend that arm across the chair, to lay his hand on my arm.

I want to put my head in my hands. I want to stop being a grown-up. I want to run away from the knowledge that this will be my last birthday with him, that he's probably not going to make his own in October. I still don't want stupid cards and a cake and a bunch of *Oh, how old are you's?* But Deven is right. I *have* to have my birthday this year.

And I have one week to remember how to celebrate.

GOOD NIGHT

*R*aina's living room has been converted to the equivalent of a hospital room. Keara's large bright-blue futon from her first college apartment is spread out like an island—where Deven can sit or lie, where people can stay next to him or just sit around the edges for visits. It can also hold his stuff—the amazing array of supplies needed for home care. Brian's—now Deven's—recliner has been moved next to the futon, a comfortable seat for a caretaker to get some shut-eye and, with the release of another button, a rocking chair to hold Deven.

People go about their business—walking over, around, and through, keeping Deven in the loop. The TV and video sit in the midst of all this, guaranteeing that there is always a sibling, cousin, grandma, auntie, friend, and, most of all, Mom around. It works well during the day, but at night Deven still wants to get into bed with Raina. His sleep is horrible. It is often hard for him to breathe, and the pain is getting substantially worse. Raina worries that he isn't honest with her when the pain changes, like he is trying to protect her from admitting things are worse. The two of them have always had an electric current connecting them. And he may well be denying increases in pain, fearing he will be hospitalized, get something worse at the doctor's office, or distress his mom in some way. He is clearly slipping.

I'm over on a Saturday morning, delivering Darren and Jade from a sleep over. Deven is pretty out of it from the painkillers, but he lets me kneel next to him and put some fingers out so he can wrap one of his fingers around and gently squeeze. Then I sit at the kitchen table while Raina measures, pours, examines the vials of medicines for the day. It's a daunting job—bubble-gum pinks, whites, yellows, and an ugly orange brown. Then there's the pill crusher and the sorting of the solid meds. The hospice nurse will be by later to take care of the ports that deliver medicine through tubes into his body. She will take Deven's pulse and temperature, listen to his lungs, and more than that listen to Raina's observations and worries. She sometimes makes helpful suggestions, but most important, she stands between Deven and hospitalization.

I want to just get up and start cleaning the kitchen, but Raina wants to do what she wants to do. Plus, she has made no secret of her opinion that I am not the world's greatest housekeeper. She holds a vial up to the light and as she stretches, her pregnancy becomes so visible and real to me in a way it hasn't yet. She's pale and holds her hand on her back for support.

"Raina, can't someone else take a night for you? You know I will. I'm sure other people will."

"No, you know that he just doesn't settle down without me. When he gets up crying, then I wonder how much sleep the other kids are getting." She finishes the last of the counters while I read a coupon mailer. Out of the blue, she says, "You know what I would love?" She asks it almost playfully.

Surprised, because she usually doesn't talk like that, I answer, "No, what would you love?"

"A big fat steak . . . with mushrooms!"

"And sour cream with some baked potato in it?" I add.

"And salad . . . rolls . . . and appetizers." She continues to spin the wish.

"Okay, stop, stop! I'm going to start eating this dish towel," I beg. "Does any place come to mind?"

"Sweetwater's. My cousin used to work there."

"Is that the one in Fairfax?"

"Yeah. It is *so* good."

"Do you think you can get someone to sit for a few hours, maybe right after Deven's dose of morphine?"

"Yeah, but how?"

"Because you've got me drooling—and remember the birthday money I got last week? Let's blow it."

She hesitates.

"C'mon, it will be two girls out on a Saturday night. . . . How long has it been?"

As she picks up the phone, she says, "I'll try my mom first."

I wave good-bye to the kids, who have settled into their video. Deven is not very alert, but I kiss him good-bye. He nods.

Thirty minutes later, I get a call back.

"My mom can do it."

"Great. When's the best time to leave?"

"How about I pick you up at eight?" Raina offers.

"My mouth is watering already."

"Just wait. This will be the best steak you've ever had," she promises.

Raina arrives with her hair pulled back and some lipstick on. She is wearing a pair of black pants, matching jacket, and red top. I've changed into a bright cotton dress with a blazer and I've actually put makeup on and mousse in my hair. With every awful thing going on, we are both of surprisingly good cheer, and there's a sense of excitement about the evening. It's a temporary suspension of reality, an unspoken agreement to allow this moment between us to be different. It's been so long since we've been alone together and even longer since we've had fun.

"You know the way, right?" she asks.

Immediately my blood pressure soars. "Raina, it's *your* place, not mine." I protest. "You know, I forget the way to *my own house.*"

"I'm messin' with you." She laughs as she slips a piece of gum in her mouth, accelerates and cruises along.

"It's *not* funny, but if you give me a piece of gum, I won't hold it against you." She reaches into her purse and tosses a piece in my direction. "I always thought I had the worst sense of direction . . . till I met you."

"Oh, I'm glad I am such a boost to your self-esteem."

She has a nice gospel tape on—not one of those walls of sound that make me feel like I'm on the express road to Hell if I don't join up now. A woman's gorgeous voice is singing about despair and pain, with simultaneous praise and thanks—a combination I never thought possible until my friendship with Raina.

"This is so nice." I prop my bare feet up against her dashboard, chomp on my gum, and relax.

"She has such a beautiful voice," says Raina.

"Yeah, Raina, so do you. . . . The first time I heard you sing, you knocked me over. I still say you could clean up—just singing at weddings a couple of hours on the weekends."

She then explains, as she always does, the flaws in her voice and the gaps in her training—all of which is probably true—but people like me wouldn't know any different. Her voice is *gorgeous*.

"Raina, all I can say is that your voice brings me closer to God."

She turns to me and smiles. There's no way she can refute that. "Well, actually, I *do* think of it every now and then. I mean right now . . ."

"Oh, you couldn't do it right now. I mean when things calm down."

"Yeah,"—she laughs—"like they ever will."

Sweetwater's is Saturday-night packed. It looks like a lot of people are waiting, and I am starving. Raina goes directly to the desk and gives her name and the time of our reservation. Then she's given one of those obnoxious little boxes that vibrate or worse to let you know your table is ready, when it really should be ready at the time you reserved it. The buzzer legitimizes lateness. Miraculously, the buzzer must have read my thoughts, and we are immediately led to an empty table in the middle of a crowded room. I should have known that trouble was a moment away. Before we sit down, Raina says politely but firmly, "I asked for a booth when I made my reservation." There is a momentary standoff between her and the hostess, who is clearly waiting for Raina to note how crowded it is and cave in. I could have saved her the trouble. Raina *wants* a booth; Raina is going to *get* a booth. The hostess excuses herself briefly and then returns, saying that if we don't mind waiting another ten minutes, we can have a booth. With one of her regal restaurant nods, Raina assents.

Ten more minutes . . . that'll be 8:40. I'm closer to bedtime than dinnertime. It turns out that the booth is worth waiting for. The menu is the size of a protest sign with print that requires a magnifying glass. Raina points out the steak dinner she's been describing all this time. We go wild and order two appetizers to split. Looking at us, no one would know the heavy burden that Raina carries. They might not be able to see the tiny boy beginning to make his presence known. They wouldn't know that I just turned forty-nine and feel like eighty, that I'm hurting from a depression I sense shadowing me again more and more ominously.

For the next four hours it is as if someone drew a protective circle around us. We bring each other up to date on our families—the brothers, sisters, their kids, her mother, my parents. They are all loved so much, but have strong personalities and enough quirks so we talk about them in sentences like "I mean, can you *believe she actually* . . ." Typical family talk. With an emphasis on funny.

The appetizers are delicious and Raina has no complaints. However, when the steaks hit the table, it's a different story. She slices into hers, then makes a face that looks like she's just swallowed a mouthful of sour milk. She starts looking around for the waiter. In the meantime I surreptitiously slice mine. It is overdone. I begin to take a bite and she stops me.

"Is that steak all right?" she demands. "It looks too well done."

"Oh, no. It's okay. I'm sure it will be fine." I brush it off.

She leans over and whispers loudly, "Did you see how much we're paying for this food?"

I nod.

"So send it back," she urges.

Oh damn, why does a perfectly good dinner have to turn into a therapy session?

The waiter comes. "Is there a problem?" he asks solicitously.

"Yes," she says in her *this-won't-do, I'm-not-satisfied* tone. "I asked for medium but this is rare." She shows the waiter, who is in absolute agreement. Her gaze turns to me, and the waiter's follows. Her look says, *If you don't say anything, I will.*

"Anything else?" he asks.

I clear my throat. "Yes . . . well . . . I think my steak is over-done. . . . I mean . . . I asked for medium, too, and this is pretty dark and . . ."

Even as I'm groveling, the guy has picked up the plate and placed it on the tray with Raina's.

"Can I bring you ladies something while you wait?"

"Complimentary?" Raina asks. *She amazes me.*

"Of course." He smiles.

"Then we'll have the same appetizers we had before." He leaves. She beams. "That wasn't too bad was it?" she says like I just got a shot at the doctor's office. "Doesn't it feel good now that you've done it?"

"No! The only reason I did it was because I had this terrible feeling that you would have done it for me and I would have felt like a little kid."

"You're right. I would have. And I would have kicked you so hard under the table . . . listen, it's your birthday dinner. I've never seen you eat steak well done. You don't like it. So you told the waiter what you wanted. You should get it." She looks like she's proud of jettisoning me out of my meek restaurant manner. Half of me could hug her and the other half could slug her.

"Yes. As long as you don't say anything about old dogs and new tricks you're okay."

The steaks, once they come, are excellent. Afterward, we share a decadent chocolate feast with so much sugar that it should be served with insulin. It's close to midnight by the time we request the bill. Between all the Diet Cokes, coffees, and chocolate, I could stay up all night, with the reassurance that I can sleep in tomorrow.

"Tomorrow." That word. Like the spell on Cinderella and in other fairy tales, the protective bubble that surrounded us begins to deflate.

It's quiet for a while.

"I hope he's asleep," she says. "The pain's getting worse."

"I know, but at least the morphine helps some."

"But he's out of it and I'm afraid of his breathing."

"He just really needs to have his pain controlled."

"I don't think he's totally honest with me about the pain," she worries.

Later, when she pulls up in front in my house we sit for a moment in silence. "Thanks for dinner, Martha," she says softly.

"It was really fun, a great way to celebrate my birthday again. Raina, I haven't laughed so hard in a long time."

"Me neither." She laughs.

"I hope it's a good night," I murmur.

"Me, too."

"I'll call you in the morning." I reach over and hug her.

"I love you."

"Love you, too," she says as she hugs me back.

Good night.

THE PASSAGE

*C*sleep till 1:00 P.M., and I'm tired from our late night—
which gives pathetic and honest evidence of the active social life I've been used to. I call Raina, sure that someone will
have skipped church to stay home with Deven. There is no answer. I get a desperate feeling. Something's wrong. No way
could they have all gone to church. Deven could not have been
moved; he couldn't have taken the motion, the action. *Oh, please
God, let him be all right. Let them be asleep over there.* I can't wait. I
need to go.

I throw on a brand-new sky blue shirt and baggy white
pants and grab a bottle of water and my cell phone, which I use
so rarely, I never remember my phone number. I tear over to
the house, knock hard on the door. There's no answer, so I sit
on the steps, although I can't sit still. In the next half hour I
watch the traffic for her car. Finally, Raina's van turns onto the
street.

She carries Deven, dressed in his gray trousers, white
shirt, and sandals. There is something wrong with the way she
is carrying him. His arms and legs are hanging, like a rag doll's,
with no energy or muscle tone. As she comes closer and I put
my hands on his head, I am disturbed by his breathing, which
is labored and rattled.

Raina smiles and says, "He said he wanted to go."

"Oh."

Inside, she sets him down gently on the futon and props
pillows under and around him. He is gray and his neck is incredibly swollen. And while he doesn't look like he's in horrible
pain, it's always hard to tell.

A little while later, after Raina has gone into the kitchen,

I get concerned by the increasing arrhythmic gurgling of his breathing and move some of the pillows so I can hold him myself.

"Hey, Jade," I call, trying to sound casual. "Will you get your mom for me?"

I can't bear what I'm about to say. "Raina, I think it's time to call the nurse from hospice."

"Why? What . . . ?"

"Well, his breathing is strained. He's starting to slip."

"Are you sure? I mean, he's really tired."

"What will it hurt?" I counter. "Has he had any fluids lately?"

"Only a little."

He gurgles and I pull him up slowly, so he can spit. He seems to get some relief once he does.

He begins to cough. Suddenly he begins to retch. I help him lean forward and he vomits a mixture of blood and bile — deep brown bloody flecks all over my new sky blue shirt. *It will never come out,* I think to myself, knowing it is a strange thought. As Raina wipes off my face and neck and shirt, someone asks if I want to change. For some reason, I can't imagine parting with this shirt right now. Raina calls the hospice nurse, and then begins calling other people. I am still holding Deven and reach over for my cell phone, which fortunately I figure out rather quickly. I dial Brian, who should be home from church by now.

"Hey, where are you?" he asks.

"Raina's."

"How's everything?"

"Not too good," I whisper as softly as I can.

He doesn't catch it. "Well, I just got back from church. I'm gonna fix some lunch and later on watch the game."

"I think it would be a good idea if you came over."

"Are things bad?" he asks.

"Uh-huh, yeah, why don't you come on over?" I suggest casually and cryptically from my end, belying the absolute desperateness of the request.

Brian arrives minutes later. He kisses Raina and sits down next to me and Deven.

"Hey, pal," he whispers, lightly stroking Deven's arm. "It's Uncle Brian."

Deven gives a small groan of recognition and then leans forward to spit out more of the bloody mucous in his throat. Raina sits down next to us with her notebook of handwritten prayers, Scriptures, reflections. She begins to pray with Deven. "You have the power, Father God. Jesus, take care of this child. Father God, heal him. Jesus, cure him of his suffering." Deven's eye's are closed, but he is intimately connected to his mother and her prayers. With each intercession, he responds with a weak, almost singsong, "ahh" or "uhh."

There is a rhythm to it. I can feel the energy of that triangle — Raina, Deven, and the God they love so passionately.

Maureen, the hospice nurse, arrives. She is upbeat and high energy. She speaks softly with Raina and then decides to make Deven more comfortable. Rather than torture him with the unbuttoning and removal of his shirt, she cuts him out of it and gets him into loose-fitting pajamas. Maureen monitors him with her stethoscope and keeps a constant check of his pulse. Jade and Darren, who hang back fearfully, are encouraged to come up if they like, to touch him lightly and talk to him softly. They do it quickly and then back away. Deven's gurgling is getting worse. It's clearly impeding his breathing and making him very uncomfortable. Maureen asks if Raina has one of those little rubber suction things you use in babys' mouths or little kids noses when they can't clear them for themselves. Odds are, there are three in the house, but, as always, when

you really need the smallest thing really badly you can't lay
your hands on it. It's sort of strange that we come in and go
out the same way—struggling for a breath, needing help with
those little rubber suction things. Keep us clear until we either
let go or start doing it for ourselves.

Brian offers to run to the store. Jade and Darren are on
their feet in a millisecond. "Can we come? Please?" Raina gives
her assent, and the threesome sets off on their mission. Once in
the van, Jade declares, "Let's get my mom a nice cold Pepsi."
Brian agrees. They have no trouble finding the rubber squeegie,
but the Pepsi proves to be quite a problem. She doesn't like ice
in her drinks, so drive-throughs are out. Jade and Darren are
determined to bring their mother something they think will
help her. It takes visits to three stores to find a cold can of
Pepsi. Brian is close to pulling what little hair he has left out of
his head. But the kids are so committed to this act of nurtur-
ance, this act of love for their mother, that he has a hard time
saying no.

One of the first relatives to arrive is Raina's aunt, Elizabeth's sister, who is a minister. She is a lovely woman with a reassuring presence. I feel relieved when I see the tears in her
eyes as she looks at Deven, like it's okay to feel sad, even
though the possibility of God's healing is still very much alive
in the room. She begins to pray over him. She begins to pray in
tongues—which I always thought would be creepy but isn't.
I'm not frightened. It is soft and lyrical, and when Raina blends
in, it sounds like the holiest of songs.

Raina sits in the recliner and Maureen helps me carry Deven
and place him in her lap. He is fairly out of it, but he acknowl-
edges his mother's presence with another audible sigh. She prays
and talks to him, touching him softly, lovingly. Relatives continue
to arrive. Her good friend Brother Eli, who lives a couple of

houses away, is over immediately with his wiry energy, his soulful presence.

Deven's breathing becomes a focal point. There is a longer time between each breath. Those of us near him find ourselves holding our breaths with his, wondering whether the next breath will come. And over a span of half an hour, one breath no longer follows the last. Raina rocks him and whispers to him and I swear she walks with him as far as she can go. I'm so glad we aren't at the hospital, where some litany of beeps would announce his death in an abrupt now-he's-here, now-he's-gone kind of way. I never truly understood the way black people sometimes used the word "passing" in place of "dying." But watching Raina and her sweet boy, I can see that this journey—this long, brutal, trying journey that they have traveled together—doesn't end with a beep. It ends with her walking with him until she offers him up to his next destination, like a mother helping her little boy make the transition to school or another place to which she cannot accompany him the whole way. Maureen listens to his heart with her stethoscope and uses her fingers to feel for the rhythm in his wrist.

"He's gone," she whispers solemnly.

Raina rocks him and weeps.

There is no hurry to do anything else.

Brian and the kids pull up and see all the people on the front lawn. Jade spots CeCe crying.

"I know what happened," Jade says, and runs into the house. Darren's eyes are full of fear and confusion. As he and Brian cross the street, he begins to cry.

The kids find their mom and brother in the recliner. Raina encourages them to come close, telling them it's okay to touch him and talk to him.

"Is he dead?" Jade asks.

"Yes, Jade, he is," her mother answers.

"He looks just like he's sleeping," Darren observes.

In one of the most difficult transitions, Maureen whispers to me about "the arrangements." I don't know what she's talking about at first, and then it clicks. *Oh God, arrangements. That means money.* I feel so angry that this is what we have to turn to with this child warm in his mother's arms. I ask Elizabeth. I ask Raina's sister Alana. Someone's going to have to talk to Raina, but not now. And what do we say? What do we do? I know she hasn't made arrangements. And I feel so stupid that I have no idea how much arrangements even cost.

James, the children's father, comes through the front door, consumed with grief. As angry as I am at him for the way he has neglected his children, they have always adored him, and he is truly bereft. He's not exactly entering friendly territory either. He gives Darren and Jade huge hugs. And then he approaches Raina and Deven. And in one of the most profoundly forgiving acts I have ever been allowed to witness, Raina holds her arms out to James. At first he doesn't know what she's doing. But she stands up, with Deven in her arms, and conveys him to his father, allowing James to take the seat she has held over the past few hours. I can't believe it, while at the same time, I can. All I know is that it is one of those truly unselfish blessings that you rarely see, let alone, perform. My friend's constant question about whether she is a good mother is answered in a second, by the extension of her arms to a man who doesn't deserve it. But I am no one to judge.

Everyone is milling about in the living room, clustering on the front lawn. Inside, we are struggling with arrangements. It's the first time I'm happy about the proliferation of cell phones. We're at work—trying to find out about the choices, the cost, and possible reductions in the fees. I get one number where someone tells me that the state will help, allocating three hundred dollars, which I say is great and then the person tells me it is under the condition that Deven be cremated, something Raina is against. The funeral home decided on is Chin's, which is what Raina wants. It is expensive, although I don't know how it compares to others. Fortunately they agree to accept a down payment, and then fairly quickly we have to come up with the rest.

We speak very frankly about how much we can contribute, beg, borrow, or steal. As I call my family members to let them know about Deven's death, I also hit them up for money. Everyone pledges something, which will go a long way toward covering the cost. There's no big deal about it, no discomfort, just the shared comfort between her sisters, her mother, Brian, and me that we can tell her she can have what she wants without worrying about the cost. Then there's the burial place, which is going to be another financial stretch. I hit up some friends. Fortunately, the cemetery people agree to a payment plan for the plot and marble that Raina thinks is manageable. Oh, to be talking about this in the midst of such grief.

It is early evening when the funeral home van shows up. James stands up with his son in his arms, and he and Raina walk Deven out to the van, with friends and relatives following in procession. The technician takes him from James and places him on a long gurney in the cavernous space. He looks so tiny. Right before the driver closes the door, Jade runs up the teddy bear she'd made for the new baby. She explains, "He'll be lonely." And she places it right next to Deven. The technician closes the door. We stand still and watch the taillights come on, and then follow them as they get smaller and smaller, before disappearing altogether.

Slowly, everyone moves inside, and an automatic prayer circle, full of sorrow and joy, coalesces in the living room.

"Thank You, Jesus. Thank You, Father God. Thank You for this child. We know he is with You. He's no longer in pain."

We are holding hands, standing shoulder to shoulder. It is hot and sweaty, yet no one wants to let go. Brother Eli leads the prayer, increasing its intensity.

"Thank You, God, for everyone here. Thank You for the love that binds us together. Thank You, Lord, thank You, Lord, thank You, Lord, thank You, Lord. Praise God. Praise Him. Praise God. Praise the Lord."

Deven has made his passage.

Good-bye, sweet boy.

WHERE HEAVEN BEGINS

Deven's island—the big blue futon, surrounded by all of the beloved toys and videos, plus the many medical supports—still dominates the living room, although now it is adrift. A room this full has never felt so empty. Raina is sitting in the recliner while people take their turns talking with her. Others, like CeCe, Deven's big cousin whom he adored and who adored him, are dealing with the eruption of sorrow alone.

Two voices approach Brian and me and ask simultaneously, "Can we spend the night?"

I immediately say, "This isn't really a night for a sleep over."

In unison, they counter very seriously, "Yes, it is." There is a fear in their eyes, a need I can't quite name.

Brian tells them that their mom would probably want them at home for the night. Of course, before it's completely out of his mouth, they've run over to Raina to ask her.

Surprisingly, she says yes. She turns to us and asks if that would be okay. "I have a couple of places to go in the morning to get some things planned and settled and it would probably be better if they weren't here," she explains.

"It's fine," I say. "They can stay as long as they need to."

Darren pulls on my arm. "Let's go now," he demands with some urgency.

Jade is in complete agreement.

"What about your clothes?" Brian asks.

Jade yells across the room, "What about my clothes?"

Doubting that laundry has been a big priority in the past few days, I suggest, "Let's not bother Mom about clothes. We'll get some out of your drawer at our house. Or tonight you can sleep in one of Keara's nightgowns and, Darren, you can sleep in one of Uncle Brian's T-shirts. Do you have any of your sleep-over pants?" I ask hoping he catches my drift.

He looks panicked.

"You know what—we have to stop at the grocery store," I add immediately. "How about I pick up some when I go in?"

Instantly relieved, he agrees. "Yeah, that's a good idea. And can we get something to eat?"

"Go kiss your mom good-bye, and we'll get you everything you need."

They hug her hard quickly, kiss her, and almost run out the front door. I blow Raina a kiss and tell her I'll see her tomorrow. By the time Brian and I have said our quick good-byes, the kids are already at our van. The impatience with which they stand there waiting makes it look like a getaway car.

"Whew, I'm glad to be out of there!" Darren exclaims.

"There were so many people and they were crying. It was terrible," Jade adds in total agreement.

We drive in silence.

"Deven died." Darren's voice comes from the backseat.

"Yeah, honey, he did."

Jade pipes up. "I don't know why they had to take him away like that."

Brian, not sure whether it was the *timing* or the *form* that bothers her says, "How do you mean?"

"He could have stayed longer and I didn't like it when they put him in that truck all by hisself," she answers.

"He'll be lonely," adds Darren.

"Do you know where they're taking him?" I ask.

Darren answers with a guess. "To get a funeral?"

"Yeah, he has to get ready for two things. One is called a viewing, where everyone comes and he's in a pretty box called a casket and he's in his best clothes with flowers and things and you can say good-bye."

"You mean we're gonna see him all dressed up and dead?"

"Yes."

"Gross."

"Well it sounds gross if you haven't seen one before, but it makes a lot of people feel better because they get to see him fixed up so he doesn't look sick anymore, just like himself."

"But he's not doing anything."

"No, he'll look like he's asleep."

"What are we going to get to eat?" asks Jade, getting down to business.

We go to the store and pretty much give in to all the kids' food choices. Darren elbows me and gives me a look that reminds me to surreptitiously get the overnight pull-up pants for five-year-olds who are, as we say, "strong, deep sleepers." Darren makes it clear that he wants to be with Jade and Uncle Brian while the food is purchased and that I should buy the pants as if he has nothing to do with them. (The self-esteem boosting on this subject has only gone so far.) I bum some money from Brian, and the whole transfer of money for goods goes well.

Once we're home I suggest, "When you guys get in your pajamas, then I'll wash your clothes so they'll be ready for you in the morning."

"Do we have to go right to bed?"

"No, we're going to eat and then watch a video," Brian says.

"What video?"

"I don't know. We'll look through what's here," I tell them.

"Then we'll watch till we're sleepy and go to bed," Brian reminds them.

"Aunt Martha . . . what if we *don't* get sleepy?"

"Well, you can read a book or something," I suggest.

I go upstairs to set up Keara's room—usually Jade sleeps in Keara's bed and Darren on a mattress on the floor. As I'm doing that, Darren silently approaches Brian, who's fixing the food at the stove.

"Hey, big guy, what's up?" he asks after feeling Darren's tug on his shirt.

"Uncle Brian, I gotta ask you something *really* important."

"What is it?"

"Can me and Jade sleep in your room tonight?"

"Well, wouldn't you be more comfortable in Keara's room, on the mattress?"

"Oh no," he answers with certainty.

"Sometimes we've had sleeping bags on your floor," he adds. "You've liked that."

"Darren, you know we'll leave the hall light on and the bathroom light. If you need us in the night you can get us."

Darren rests his head against Brian's hip. "I need to be with you *all* of the night."

Brian almost loses his grip on the frying pan, gulping back

the rush of tears that are just waiting for release. "And I need you, too, pal."

Darren gives Brian a quick hug. "I better go tell Aunt Martha that we've changed our plans."

"Yeah, you do that," Brian says to this child who never fails to make him smile.

Jade, Darren, and I fix up a space on the floor of our bedroom for them to sleep. They are happy to sacrifice comfort for closeness. And, frankly, so am I. After consuming a disgusting combination of junky food, we settle down with unanimous agreement to watch *Baby's Day Out*, the unlikely sounding movie that was one of Deven's all-time favorites. I love this movie. A rich and pampered baby is kidnapped and in his escape he revisits all of the adventures from his favorite book, *Baby's Day Out*. It's a series of near misses, with bad guys being outwitted by a toddler, and it's truly hilarious. As we watch, we all register our physical fatigue. By the time it's finished, it's quite late, and Brian announces, "Lights out."

We get them kissed and cuddled and settled. We open the bedroom door, turn on the hall and bathroom lights, and make it clear that if they wake up, they can just come over to us and we'll help them get back to sleep.

Brian turns out the lights.

I remind them to say their prayers.

"God bless Mommy and Grandma and Deven. And give him the right food because he's a picky eater and let him have good clothes — like in style. And now that he's in Heaven You've *got* to make sure he's got sunglasses. He has to have his shades!"

Darren affirms her. "Amen!"

We lie there in silence, four people in a small room, reflecting in the quiet on the things that light and noise helped us avoid.

Darren pipes up. "Uncle Brian, how do you know where the sky ends and Heaven begins?"

"Well, pal, that's a tough one. I think we could look and look and look, and it would still be sky. Heaven is so special that we can't see it till we get there."

"Like Deven. He's in Heaven," states his twin.

Jades adds, "I'm sure he's in Heaven."

Brian and I agree. "And he's not sick and nothing hurts, and he is perfectly happy," says Brian.

More silence.

A few minutes later. Darren asks, "Uncle Brian, you know how they say that Jesus is everywhere? Well, what do they do, Xerox Him or something?"

I can feel Brian next to me suppressing a laugh. "I think it means He is so powerful and so amazing that for everyone who needs Him, He's right there, even if you can't see Him."

"He can see *you*," Darren adds.

"Yeah, pal," Brian says with tears in his voice. "He can."

"He can *always* see you."

THE NEWSPAPER

DEVEN RYAN GRANT
Age 5, "Our Wonder"
Went home to Glory, Sunday, August 26, 2001

We find great comfort knowing that he is walking on streets of gold and rejoicing. Loved ones include his mother, Raina; sister, Jade (7); twin brother, Darren; father, James; half sister, Jennifer (3); grandmothers; and many beloved aunts, uncles, and cousins. Deven delighted in stories; cowboy boots; make-believe; *GQ*-style cooking; *Barney*; and *Veggie Tales*'s Larry-Boy, who was "the man." He enjoyed calling the shots, wrestling with Darren, and hearing Jade read. He loved praying with Mommie most of all. His steadfast faith made him wise beyond his years and touched everyone he met. "Our Wonder" fought a good fight.

The Washington Post, August 28, 2001

*D*arren excitedly runs up to me with a copy of *The Washington Post*. "Deven got hisself in the paper!" he announces with pride.

9-11

I wake up on a day that everyone but the Grinch would agree is beautiful. It's the kind of early autumn day you know is gorgeous just by the way the light tilts into your bedroom and the purity of the sunlight that boldly breaks through your blinds and reminds you that summer's end is not entirely bad.

It was after another in a series of several weeks of long nights, obsessing, twisting, and kicking in bed until Brian groggily but politely suggested I find another sleeping place. At about 5:00 or 6:00 A.M., I usually succumb to the kind of sleep I deserved to start getting at midnight.

Brian rushes into the room, turns on the TV, and announces urgently, "They bombed the World Trade Center." It all sounds vaguely familiar and I'm in no mood to walk down disaster memory lane.

"I know," I croak and pull the covers over my head and go back to sleep.

"And they just hit the Pentagon—" He turns up the volume. I am halfway between a hangover of nightmares and a far worse reality. I fumble with my glasses.

"Who?" I manage to get out.

"No one knows." He hands over two cans of Coke—the only substance known to man that can rescue me from a miserable night and plunge me into the consciousness required for day.

"Oh God, Keara!" I cry, picturing her in her Brooklyn apartment.

Brian reminds me she's studying in Sweden.

"Oh right! She's there. We've got to call. She must be frantic." I dial the number over and over, but I can't get through. They're five hours ahead, so she must know. She's probably trying to call us.

The Pentagon! Two miles away. Blown up! I always thought we were safe living near the national monuments, especially in the shadow of that symbol of defense.

I call my parents, who are fine. Images and memories flash in my head like on TV. Brian's father spent his whole career at the Pentagon in the office of the Chief of Naval Operations. I taught a couple of Catholic University graduate psychology courses there, always struggling to negotiate the astounding layout of ring within ring. My "classroom" was always a bit forbidding, located in some admiral's conference room, the head of the table flanked by all kinds of flags. Everyone but me wore some uniform, which I never could decode in terms of branch or rank.

On a more banal level is the mall, "our mall," the Pentagon City Mall—across the street—the locus of many special treats as well as daily necessities.

How can this be?

"Oh God," Brian and I say almost in unison, "Raina!"

"What time is it?" I ask Brian.

"The kids are in school," I figure. "Let me call her." I put my money on her not being home. Not alone. Not since Deven died two weeks ago and the kids started school a week ago. She's been having a hard time staying home. It has been years since she's been alone. And even though she has an active, healthy son in utero as a companion, it's just not the same as the past eight years of her life. I call her home anyway. Just the answering machine. Next her cell phone. It rings and rings, and when she finally answers, the static is overwhelming.

"Raina?"

"Martha?"

"Oh, thank God. Are you all right? Where are you?"

"I'm in bad traffic."

"Where?"

"Guess."

"Near the Pentagon?"

"Yeah, and I can't really see anything over there but horrible smoke."

"Do you know what's happened?" I ask.

"Yeah, I was doing some errands and I was gonna go to Costco and maybe Pentagon City. But then I turned on the radio, and now I'm just trying to get the kids. I have got to get my kids. They have a recording on when you call the school."

"Listen, I'm not gonna keep you on. Call when you and the kids get home."

Two hours later, she calls. "Hey, it's me."

"Are you home?"

"Yeah. I have the kids. We've been trying to remember if Keara's in Sweden yet."

"She is safe and sound. Remember, she left right before Deven?"

"Praise the Lord!" She sighs with relief.

"You said it." I surprise myself with my automatic response.

"Did the school know what was going on?"

"Yeah. The lady at the desk said their policy was that they weren't closing down and they didn't want parents to pick their kids up early. I almost lost it."

"Oh, I can imagine," I say, trying to picture the scene.

"I said to her, 'Give me my kids. I'm taking them home with me *now*.' I mean, Martha, what would you say? I'm about a mile and a half from the Pentagon—a straight shot. I was so scared."

"You probably scared the hell out the school secretary."

Her voice is shaking as she describes it. I can picture every fiber of her taking on the Mother Tiger role at that school. Most people at school don't know about Deven and that he died just before school started. It makes things so much harder.

"Well, I think this lady could tell that I wasn't leaving without the kids, so she got them," Raina reports with momentary pleasure that then switched quickly to the universal horror of the day. She wants to shield them from the full weight of the news by structuring the day with videos and games. "What am I going to tell them?" she wonders, expecting no answer.

Keara gets through to us in a terrible connection, frantic about her friends in the neighborhood and those in New York. She already feels a terrible guilt about not being here—Deven's death and now this. I don't say it, but for the first time in her life, I thank God she is so far away.

SLIPPING

*I*t's hard to escape your fate. We grow up coming to believe that we can control, should control, ourselves. For the second time in three weeks I am besieged by a vicious anxiety and depression that kicks in ten seconds after I wake up. When I am absent, it is present. When I am present, it is absent. I am losing all strength and vitality. My optimism about the future is gone. I would kill for a decent night's sleep and a day's alertness. And all I can do is cry and pray, "God, please don't let me go back to that place where death looks more beautiful than life, where putting one foot in front of the other is a day's work, where combing my hair and getting dressed seem an unfamiliar process and interactions with people deserve Academy Awards for acting." I'm afraid I won't make it back out this time.

Jeremy, my doctor, says that I'm certainly reacting to the events of the past few months—Deven's illness and death, 9-11, Keara's moving to Sweden. But he's also concerned that my medicine needs adjusting and sends me for some blood tests.

CHICKEN LITTLE

*M*y own sense of personal invincibility was shattered several years ago by a tornado in my mind that both caught me up in its whirlwind and laid me flat for too long a time. And now the naive belief that age should regulate the order of living and dying, making a child's death inexplicable, a moment when God looked away, and someone tossed the divine deck in the air—twos trump the aces, and jokers rule.

But I have never questioned the security of my surround-ings. Anyone who sees my three-bedroom brick colonial would agree that it needs work, but it still allows me to sleep with the full knowledge that somehow the roof, walls, windows, and foundation will hold together—and they do. Even though it's allowed greedy intruders in twice; even though it's impossible for our Volvo to retain a new hubcap for more than several weeks; I am not consumed with worry about my basic care or safety. I could extend those assurances about my street and neighborhood.

Whenever I see the stark, incomprehensible horror of di-saster, national or international, there is always a split screen in my mind that allows me to view entire villages wiped out, to hear of death tolls in hundreds and thousands, to register the general horror, and to think "My God, those poor people"— but that side of the screen never overwhelms the safe side. It never allows the disaster to challenge my own sense of safety in the places—house and country—that I call home.

Countries have been screaming, crying, and pleading for help from us for years. The screens *they* look at aren't split. It is one horror with no alternative, no respite. We can finally believe what they've been telling us.

Chicken Little was right.

The sky *is* falling.

FEELING LOUSY

I am fading, slipping into the arms of a depression that has been lurking but that I've been able to shake off somehow. Lately, though, it's been harder. I'm falling farther and farther behind, slowing down. I know this territory. I withdraw from other people as much as possible, not wanting to impose myself on them and also not be embarrassed by myself, for myself. Sleep is a stranger.

My family knows. They also know that when my work slows down, so does the money coming in. I'm really close to shaking the family tree to see who can front me some money until my next royalty check.

I'm afraid Raina and the kids are starting to pick up on the way I'm fading out. I've been turning down their invitations, not stopping by as much. I let the machine pick up most of my calls. Jeremy, my doctor, keeps telling me not to automatically jump to conclusions that this depression is as bad as the last. I just have to hold on while the new medicines kick in.

While Brian and I were away at my doctor's, Raina has stopped by. There is a card and flowers on our front steps. She knows I get such a kick out of flowers. I choose a card for someone in less than sixty seconds, but Raina really pays attention. The card she leaves says, *May the morning sunlight warm and renew you. May afternoon moments of quiet fill your heart with peace. May the evening hours bring you comfort and rest. And may you always know how very much you're loved.* Raina added, *We love you so much. God bless you and keep you.* It's sort of Celtic. I sit down on the steps and burst into tears.

After I pull myself together, I call to thank her. Still sniffling, I'm sure I'll get the machine. But Raina picks up.

"I got the card and the flowers, and it was such perfect timing because we just got back from the doctor's . . . and it was so
hard. . . ." I start crying all over again.

"Martha, what's the matter?" Raina asks. "It's going to be
okay."

"I am so scared." I sniffle a few more times and then shift
gears. "How are *you*?"

"Well," she answers hesitantly, "I just found out my electric
got cut off."

"Are you kidding? Did they give you notice?"

"Well, they sent a bill, but, no, they didn't send some threat
that they're going to cut me off. They just did it."

"So what do you have to do to get it turned back on?"

"Deliver sixty-four dollars and forty-three cents to the office before the end of the day. The thing is, I deposited my first
check from the new job, but the bank said because it was a new
account, it would take a few days to clear."

"Give me a few minutes and I'll call you back," I promise.
"You know I have the can I save my quarters in? We may be
able to make it."

"Okay."

I spill everything out onto the bed. I've got it! It's not all
rolled, but I've got it.

"Come on over," I call her. "We've got it." I pile it all into an
old makeup bag.

She comes by, breathless and relieved, and when she sees
the makeup bag says jokingly, "Hey, this is nice. Can I keep it?"

We both crack up, despite the way we both started out
that day.

She runs out to pay the bill before closing.

I put my flowers in a vase. And take a nap.

✿   ✿   ✿

There's really never a question of whether I am enough or have enough to share with someone else. If I have anything, *anything*, I have something. A card, a laugh, a makeup bag with change. Whatever. I can make it enough.

OVERDUE

*T*here's *still* no baby, although what right do I have to complain? I'm not the one overflowing, more than ready after nine months of transformation. There is such a burden on Raina—a prelude to another huge life change. Another life. It's one thing to have the innocence of a first and even subsequent pregnancies. No one goes in thinking that the rules will be anything other than what they've always been. Child is born—mother lives, child lives; mother dies, child lives. It is a sorrowful parade, a hole never to be filled. These reversals—when a child's ticket on earth is punched way too early—are beyond huge. They're craters, ground zero, still smoldering months after the explosion. Nothing will ever be the same again.

Josiah . . . the child to be. Surprising, wrenching, growing while his mother was not. As if there was some finite energy between Deven and the unseen one in the womb. Raina began to show as Deven began to fade, to lose touch with his world as the baby began to flutter and float, reminding Raina that he was exactly where he was supposed to be. The baby swam and Deven sank, pushing away his brother and sister with an economy of movement, of sound, of change. While Josiah was on automatic pilot inside Raina, she gave all to Deven—every waking hour, until all hours became waking hours.

HERE COMES THE SON

It's Elizabeth's birthday, December 17. Raina is in labor, has been for about six hours, since the middle of the night. Eli, who is her coach, has been with her, along with her sister Kendra, and has maintained high energy through the night. I get a couple of calls but I am in such bad sleep from new medicines that make me drowsy or wired, depending on the time of day, that I can't take them. Brian gets the updates.

I am finally sleeping, but it's a drugged sleep and I cannot for the life of me wake up, get ready for business, and get to the hospital. I figure I'm more important later in the process, anyway. But there's a lingering guilt that I am deserting her.

At about 5:00 A.M. Kendra calls and insists that I come — Raina keeps asking for me. Brian fixes me a cup of turbo coffee. It helps, although I am still so out of it, he decides to drive me to the hospital. We pull up and it's too familiar — the same place I was hospitalized for depression.

We run up to Labor and Delivery. I'm told she's in Room 72. I find every number in the seventies, but I can't find her room. Then I hear her — whimpering, crying — and I hear Eli's upbeat voice urging her on.

The birthing room is spacious. There's a baby area in the corner. The place is well stocked — belts, catheters, monitors. It reminds me that there isn't a damn thing natural about this. Perhaps that's why Eli wants out now. He was comfortable with her through the long night, through her contractions and the discomfort, but when it comes to getting down to the nitty-gritty — I don't know if it's an issue of modesty or some parameters of his faith about what you do and don't do with women to whom you aren't married—he is ready to retire to the waiting room. Dignity is easily sacrificed in these birthing rooms— having to lift your nearly naked, tired body up, so the nurse can change those big blue pads under you, while pillows, white blankets, and sheets are placed and displaced. Raina begins to cry when she sees me.

"Oh, you poor baby," I tell her while I smooth her hair.

Kendra rubs one leg and I do the other. I take a washcloth and wipe her forehead. Raina is exhausted.

A nurse comes in to check her. Unfortunately, she has not dilated much more than the six centimeters she's been for over an hour. The nurse adjusts the fetal monitor belt, and pats Raina. "Things have slowed down, but don't lose heart—they'll get going again." Raina gets an epidural, which helps the pain, but the intense pressure is extremely uncomfortable.

It's then that it hits me. I've never coached anyone through childbirth. My own delivery was a C-section after never dilating more than two centimeters.

"Miss Raina," I tell her between contractions. "I don't know nothin' 'bout birthin' babies."

She gives me a wan smile. "Ha, ha," she mutters.

What I don't tell her is that I've been trying to make up for it by catching a few of those baby shows on TV, you know, *The Baby Story*, where they follow a woman through her pregnancy and then really zoom in for the misery of labor. They don't shy away from the pushing and delivery either. It's simultaneously painful from an empathic point of view and very useful from an educational point of view.

"You're telling me this *now*?" she jokingly complains.

"Yeah. It will be okay. I promise."

❊ ❊ ❊

Over the next hour, Raina's discomfort escalates enough for her to ring for the nurse.

"I was right," she affirms, after examining Raina again. "Time to call Dr. Salinas."

Raina is relieved. Dr. Salinas delivered Jade and the twins. She was so hoping that she'd be four for four. Tall, blond, all-business Dr. Salinas comes in and asks Raina if she's ready to see her son. A second's look at her answers that question. She checks the fetal monitor and is not fully happy with what she sees, but doesn't look too distressed.

"Raina, I want you to take a little oxygen," she tells her. "It will help with the pushing." Raina breathes directly from the mask for a few minutes. Then the doctor hands the mask to Kendra and tells her to hold it near Raina, so the air is always on call. All of a sudden, we're in action. The nurse is getting the stirrups in position. We are lifting Raina's legs and supporting them with pillows. Between the nurse, doctor, Kendra, and me, we get Raina into perhaps the most revealing, humble, basic of basic positions in life.

"Okay," Dr. Salinas announces. "We're ready."

I always love the royal "we" doctors use when it comes to childbirth. It makes you want to rip off the head of anyone who says it and hand it to them on a silver platter.

"It's time to push." She instructs Kendra and me to count with the pushing. One to ten.

I'm looking at Raina head-on. The baby is engaged. In a little while, a whole infant will emerge through that bulging space that is already working, contracting, and ready for the showdown, requiring every ounce of strength Raina has, along with the help her impatient little boy will add to his own quest to come out, to become hers.

The nurse leans her forward.

"Push!" the doctor says. "Push!"

"One, two, three, four, five, six, seven, eight, nine, ten!"

By the time we get to "four" I am so overwhelmed by the screaming fatigue, the pressure, and the pain that I can't say six, seven, eight, nine, ten fast enough. So far, I'm not much of a coach. Kendra and I get it together and count rhythmically. Raina needs oxygen every now and then.

"There's fetal distress," the doctor observes. "Raina, be prepared for a C-section."

"But I delivered twins vaginally," she protests.

"It's not you. It's just that we're not moving along fast enough. Don't worry, we're still going to push."

Dr. Salinas suctions out blood from around Raina's vagina. Then a lot of mucous becomes disengaged. Raina gives two big pushes, and suddenly a cone-shaped, hairy round thing bursts out.

"Stop pushing for a minute, Raina."

"Is everything okay?"

"Everything's fine."

"No C-section?"

"No C-section. We're going to have you give one more good push when I tell you, and you will have your son."

She doesn't even make it to the count of five when a slippery, wrinkled, pale, almost white body slithers out into hands ready to catch him. Dr. Salinas lays him on Raina's belly while she examines Raina. The wormy red-gray braid of a cord connects them as Raina delivers the placenta that sustained his life for over nine months. They cut the cord and whisk the baby over to the table in the corner. He makes no sound. We are all silently waiting for him to announce his presence on this earth.

The nurse suctions out his nose and mouth, and for a moment I remember Deven's last moments, and similar actions.

But this new being—cleared of all the fluids of his birth—
bursts out with a wail. And it is such a claim on life, on Raina,
on all of us welcoming him into the world.

As Raina cradles him, I run to the waiting room. It is a
blessing to be crying tears of joy.

Eli and Brian jump up as I approach.

"Josiah Daniel Grant is here," I announce between gulps
for air.

We embrace, laughing, crying, Eli praising the Lord.

Josiah Daniel Grant.

He is so lucky.

We are luckier.

FIREFLIES

*I*t's been a too long a time since we've taken a trip with the
kids out to Rachel and Greg's. With depression dogging
me for months, I use the weekends to withdraw and collapse.
Raina has been busy with Josiah. Greg and Rachel have been
in way over their heads as well. But the kids, Darren especially,
want to see "Mr. Greg."

After fifteen minutes in the car they start complaining about
the distance. When Brian warns how much time we have left,
they start asking for music. Darren gets his wish (and Brian's)
as they listen to their Celtic wild men, Great Big Sea. They sing
out loud, while Jade wonders with me what school next year
will be like. It's a hot day, but absent the usual wretched humidity of the area.

Brian is meeting Greg, my father, and my sister Priscilla to
play nine holes of golf on the course that adjoins Greg and

Rachel's house. They have two carts, and even with that, Brian is prepared for the game to take forever. When I ask him to describe the level players they are, he answers, "hackers," which isn't very good. It's not clear if there is anything worse.

Jade and Darren love their usual countdown of the huge mosques, churches, and temples that set the stage for Rachel's development. When we get close, Brian has to remind them to stay buckled in. He's afraid of them being so excited, they'll try getting out and actually hurt themselves. As we pull up, four-year-old Sean is driving his little motorized tractor slowly down their long driveway.

"What's he wearing?" Jade asks, which is an excellent question.

As we get closer, we can see that he's got on his cowboy boots, a pirate hat with a huge purple plume, and a stuffed parrot somehow affixed to his shoulder.

"He looks bigger," Darren comments. "What's that he's riding?"

Brian tells him it's a kid's tractor, sort of like the tractor that Greg uses to mow the lawn. I can tell Darren can't wait to get his hands on it.

"Where's Tori and Gracie?" asks Jade, searching the yard.

"Let's go inside and see."

Sean gets off the tractor and greets Darren as "Deven" — which surprisingly Darren doesn't correct. He goes immediately in search of Mr. Greg and hugs him. Greg lifts him up, and Darren beams when he says how big he's gotten.

"I'm strong, too. You should see me play basketball."

"Do you want to play? I can do it for a few minutes before we go play golf."

Darren is breathless as he follows Greg into the garage, which to Darren is sports wonderland—with every piece of sports equipment for kids of all ages mounted on walls or hung from the ceiling. They grab two basketballs and head out to the driveway, where Greg has a real hoop, and the flat driveway has lots of room to approximate a court. Darren is dwarfed by the height of the hoop, but when he starts to play, he is striking in his ability to land one basket after another. Greg is amazed. My father and sister Priscilla arrive, and the motley golfing foursome is off to do their damage, leaving behind one unhappy basketball player. Sean takes this as his opportunity to be accepted by Darren as a "big boy."

"Hey, Deven," he yells, "you wanna play?"

They get down two lacrosse sticks and Sean tries to explain lacrosse to Darren. Darren decides the rules aren't relevant, and somehow between them, they work out a game of sorts.

Inside, with Tori down the street playing with a friend, Gracie is licking her chops for Jade. "Jade, want to do arts and crafts or play with dolls or dress up or watch a video?" Jade is flattered to be courted like this and takes right to it. They sit down in the playroom and make posters using markers and stickers. Gracie is really anxious for Jade to pledge her loyalty before Tori breezes in and, in a snap, has Jade following her.

Rachel and I visit at the table in the kitchen—the epicenter of the house. Tori comes back and somehow, the girls do well together. Jade loves being the center of attention, for once.

"We have to keep an eye out for the guys," Rachel reminds us. We plan to be there for the foursome as they struggle their way to the third green. I do a quick check for the kids that are my responsibility. No Darren.

"Sean, have you seen Darren?"

"He died."

Oh God. Jade is right there.

Gracie yells, "Se-an! Deven's the dead one, not Darren."

"Uh-uh."

"*YES!* Ja-ade? Aren't I right?"

Rachel and I stare at each other, horrified.

Jade, who has been engrossed in poems from *Where the Sidewalk Ends* by Shel Silverstein, looks up casually. "What?"

Gracie begins to repeat, and Rachel cuts in, "*Darren* is playing," hoping she gets the point across.

Jade is totally confused, but at least the facts are now clear.

Rachel goes to look outside for Darren and returns with a shrug as she runs upstairs to check the kids' rooms. On the way down she spots him around the corner in the living room, where no one goes. There is Darren, sitting in the middle of the couch, still and quiet.

"Darren, are you okay?" Rachel asks.

"I'm resting. It's so quiet here," he tells Rachel. "Is it all right if I stay here awhile?"

"Yeah, honey, you can stay as long as you want. Do you want me to come get you when the golfers come by?"

"Yes, please."

She leaves him in the living room.

Tori yells out, "Here they come!"

We all run out to the backyard and up the hill to the green. The grass is delicious under our bare feet, and we jump up and down, applaud, and act like total idiots as the two carts approach. A couple of the players already look finished. We present them with cold drinks, and they give the kids a short experience of the golf cart. Then Brian and Greg let Darren and Sean take a couple of swings with their clubs. They take off again and, from the looks of them, Rachel and I are pretty sure we won't be seeing them for hours.

Dinner will go on — on time.

The boys are now united in their desire to play golf. I take

plastic fast-food cups and find some kids' golf clubs in the
garage. The boys take to it really well and it occupies them until dinner.

We have to eat fast, Rachel tells us, because it's almost
"firefly time." There are a couple of firefly catchers and jars,
with fresh grass, awaiting sunset. We gather on the green;
shoeless kids, hands full of nets and jars, and eager for the first
sighting. The sun begins to set, leaving slowly, one color trailing the next, a palette of pastels impossible to replicate. To our
back the moon is rising, always surprisingly huge and translu-
cent. The children run and shriek as they spot flashes of light.
Every now and then, they capture one and hold it up for admi-
ration. Rachel and I stand on the cusp of the green. We clap
our hands and giggle at these children and at our memories of
ourselves as children and the same thrills in the same brief window of time on summer evenings.

Out of nowhere, there's a huge burst of fireworks—a surprise. We can't figure out where or why they are here, but
those questions don't matter much. The kids are drawn to
Rachel and me. We stand together, touching and watching.
With each burst, there are exclamations: "Wow!" "Look at that
one."

Grace is so full of joy, saturated in the absolute moment,
she yells out, "I love this day!"

Tori puts her arm on Darren's shoulder, "Deven would
love this if he could see it." Immediately she adds, "But I guess
he can. . . ."

Darren thinks about it. "Well, he can't actually *see* it with
his body, because he's dead . . . but his spirit and soul are alive,
so he can see it that way. He can see everything."

"Oh okay," replies Tori.

They stand shoulder to shoulder in silence as the fireworks
fade and end.

I feel blessed to have witnessed all of this beauty, this meeting of minds, of souls so simple yet so profound. I'm with Gracie. I love this day, too.

The Place We Land

$\mathcal{I}$t seems so long since we've been to the cemetery. Raina says she hasn't visited nearly as much as she expected to, either. When Deven died I envisioned myself at his grave daily in a desperate attempt to sustain some sense of connection. Instead, I have avoided it. My most frequent and lame excuse is that the marker isn't in yet. In the Pleasant Valley Cemetery the markers are all flat and similar in size and composition, just like in Gate of Heaven Cemetery, where Jane and Ben, Brian's parents, are buried. Until now, that style has been my preference. There is a gentle order, a peaceful symmetry that allows quiet reflection for mourners and visitors.

But now I prefer the less orderly cemeteries with their wildly different testimonials: sculpted angels guarding each side of a grave, a bronzed statue of a little boy kneeling in prayer at the resting place of a child, the huge mausoleums with families together, marble benches for sitting and contemplating loved ones, plants constant or changing with the seasons, overgrown or perfectly tended shrubs, small or imposing trees.

Without the marker, without the grass grown in, without even the remotest certainty that I am near Deven's grave, I long for the slightly overgrown, highly individualistic places that cradle the remains of my ancestors in New England. There are all kinds of quirky, beautiful, or spiritual anchors in those places. Raina has been assured that Deven's marker will be in by his birthday. I automatically say, "That's good," like it will make a big difference. To be honest, though, my infrequent visits are probably related less to *where* he is buried than the fact that he is buried *at all*.

I call Raina on the morning of the twenty-sixth, the anniversary of Deven's death.

"Hey, Martha." She sounds tired and hassled.

"Brian and I woke up thinking of you guys today."

She sighs. "I want to get over to the cemetery."

I'm not sure how far to push or back off. "Yeah, we're thinking of going, too."

Silence.

I add, "We didn't know maybe if you'd want to go together."

She brightens up. "It sounds great to me . . . but I told the kids we'd be going as a family, and I just want to make sure it's okay with them. You know what I mean?"

"Raina, it's fine. . . . *Anything* that will help . . . ," I insist. "I mean even if you want us to take care of Josiah so you can go . . . anything."

"Kendra thought Jah Nel started school today instead of next week, and she's already gone to work, so I've got her, too. . . . Hold on. . . ."

She walks into the living room and poses the question about our coming with them. I feel nervous, like I've been really presumptuous. Facts are facts. We aren't family. Even though it feels like we are.

Suddenly I hear Darren shout, "Aunt Martha and Uncle Brian, yay."

Jade yells, "Yes. Yes. Yes!"

Raina walks back into the kitchen with the phone. "Did you hear that?"

"Yeah, but, Raina, is it all right with you?"

"Oh, yeah. Can we take your van?"

"No problem. . . . We can also give you some time alone at the grave if you want it."

"I was thinking about having a picnic, but I didn't know about Jah Nel being here, and now the thought of the store is just too much."

"We could do pizza or something right afterward," I suggest, "at a restaurant, your place, our place . . . whatever."

"Your place," she decides. "That's a great idea. We'll be over soon."

I salvage remnants of several vases of flowers left over from my birthday, yielding enough for a small bouquet for the grave. Since the day is already hotter than hell, Brian fills a small cooler with cans of lemonade, soda, and grapes.

Raina drives over with Jade, Darren, Josiah, and their five-year-old cousin Jah Nel. Earlier in the week, in preparation for school, I had put together little gifts for Darren and Jade. For Darren, I found a blue chrome "space pen" I got for Christmas one year. It writes upside down, which I thought was very cool until I read that instead of spending millions trying to develop such a writing instrument, the Russians just sent their astronauts into space with a bunch of pencils. There was also a beautiful clipboard made of different kinds of wood and some poster paper. For Miss Jade, I found a handmade wooden pen that disappears into its own wooden box and a pretty journal. I wrote them each a letter, wrapped everything in colorful tissue, and slid all of it into the decorative gift bags, which the kids always think are so special.

In Keara's room I found that incredibly annoying Taco Bell stuffed dog—that one that says, "I theeenk I'm eeeeen love. . . ." Josiah gets such a kick out of it when he comes over, and fortunately he can't yet find the button that makes it talk. With

Raina's five-minute notice about Jah Nel, I put together a little plastic container with six quarters, two new pencils with birds and flowers on them, and a fancy hotel soap in a small Godiva chocolate box and bow.

For Raina, Keara and I assembled a little scrapbook before she returned to New York, with pictures from my birthday party last week. Keara took a lot of shots of Raina and the kids, as well as Tori, Gracie, Sean and some of just "the girls" together. She has a great eye, and her photographs are terrific. By design or accident, Raina and her kids all wore white, which made for wonderful photos. Josiah's hair was plaited back; Raina and Jade both wore their long hair in ponytails.

Darren had to be coaxed into shots with "all those girls" and deigned to pose a couple of times. The boy has never taken a bad picture, so even the staged looks came out well. In the little scrapbook I wrote at the beginning "Life ends" and then on the next page "And life goes on," followed by the joyous pictures.

An hour later, Raina drives over, then everyone piles into our van. Raina is up front with Brian. Jade and I reach all the way to the bench seat in the third row to get Josiah secured into his car seat and then buckled into the van. It's an endeavor that requires gymnastic skills that left me long ago. When the click of the seat belt corresponds to a snap I feel in my lower back, I know I'm in trouble.

Jade and Jah Nel settle into the back row with Josiah. Darren has quietly claimed the cushy seat in the second row, leaving me on the floor next to him. Once we get going, Brian and Raina talk softly up front and the kids clamor for their gifts. I warn them of their high "boring" potential, given how much they resemble fancy school supplies. But they go over surprisingly well—except with Jah Nel, who looks perplexed at the difference between her cousins' gifts and hers and announces urgently, "Aunt Martha, there's a problem."

Alarmed because I haven't been paying much attention to the backseat, I twist around and ask urgently, "What, honey? What's the matter?"

"My presents aren't very good," she says seriously, as if she is stating evidence at a trial. "I thought you would want to know."

In the midst of trying out her new pen, Jade gets a flash of oldest-child morality. "Jah Nel," she scolds, "that is very ungrateful. I'm telling Grandma!"

Jah Nel is undeterred. "I'm grateful. I said thank you." However she just can't stop herself there. "But it's still true — you and Darren got better presents."

Darren is absorbed with brushing up on his writing on the new clipboard. Josiah, contender for Best Baby Disposition of All Time, is giving the Taco Bell dog a good going over — with the beginnings of his little Chiclet teeth.

"Jah Nel . . . ," I say contritely, "y'know I didn't know you were coming till five minutes before you showed up and since everyone else was getting a gift, I wanted you to have something, but I just didn't have time. So I put your stuff together fast."

"Oh," she says obviously surprised that I actually confessed to my crappy present giving.

"Aunt Martha . . ."

"Yes, Jah Nel."

"I have a good idea. When we get back to your house why don't you just give me more quarters."

God, little kids wear me down.

"Okay, Jah Nel — when we get back I will put three more quarters in the container. That's my final offer."

"Okay."

Case closed.

Raina must have overheard a little of this, because she

reaches behind and grabs my arm. "I love my pictures." She shows a picture of Josiah to Brian.

Brian's voice gets hoarse when I hear him say, "Wouldn't Mr. Deven have gotten a kick out of him." Darren and I are both eavesdropping. Raina starts to sniffle. She's looking straight ahead and crying. Brian looks straight ahead driving, and extends his arm to stroke hers.

Darren leans over to me and whispers loudly, "My mom is having a moment to herself." If he wasn't so damn serious, he would be funny.

"Well, even though I'm only the mother of *one* child, I know how important it is for mothers to have moments to themselves," I try to reassure him.

He ponders that a moment, but takes exception, "Yeah, but my mom always *cries* in *her* moments."

"Sometimes, especially when life is really hard, crying can help you get the hurt out so you can start to feel better. I know what I'm saying probably sounds like boring grown-up talk—"

"No," he interrupts, "I get it." He leans close and whispers, "*I cry.*"

"Me, too."

"Does Uncle Brian?"

"Yeah. Uncle Brian cried right before you guys got to our house today."

"How come?"

He was looking at that picture of you and Deven goofing around with those long black gloves and the T-shirts and those weird shades. At first he laughed, but then he felt how much he misses Deven, and I saw him in his study holding the picture and wiping his eyes."

"Oh."

"What do you cry about?" I ask.

"I wish we had Deven back and I wish Mom wasn't sad."

I point to the clipboard, paper, and pens I gave him. "Hey, maybe you could draw a picture of what you're feeling."

Damn, I'm thinking, *that's such a child-shrink thing to say.*

To my surprise, he looks satisfied and whips out the paper and upside-down-writing pen,

"Aunt Martha," he asks, "does Heaven start with a *H*?"

We pull into Pleasant Valley and find the general area of Deven's gravesite. As we spill out of the van, each person stakes out a different place. The number of new plots, combined with the drought's influence on struggling grass, makes it tough to find the right one. Jade walks over to a very dry rectangle and confidently plants herself there. "Here he is," she yells out. "Come on over."

No one else is convinced. It is hot and humid. I'm carrying Josiah in his car seat. He gets heavier by the moment. We all shift and stand around uncertainly. Darren runs to another spot and yells out, "No, you guys, here he is."

I give in to gravity and set Josiah down. "I thought it was closer to the tree," I offer.

"Deven is here," Jade insists, planting herself on the grave.

Raina and Brian decide to take the quick drive over to the office. Within minutes, Mrs. Butler has accompanied them back and confirms that Jade is right. She is thrilled with herself.

We settle down on the site, lining ourselves around the rectangle, breaking out the lemonade. And for a little while we are each lost in our own memories, our own laughter, our own sorrow. Raina smoothes the dirt, silently stroking it back and forth. Sweet Josiah splashes the air with his hands and feet, gurgling at the true delight at just being around. "Da-da-da-da-da," he sings and looks puzzled but pleased at his ability to make everyone laugh.

I sit in a position that used to be so automatic but has become infrequent—cross-legged, with my arms stretched out behind, leaning backward.

Darren walks over and despite the ninety-degree-plus temperature and ferocious humidity, he settles into the chair seat I've made with my body. This makeshift chair was the one that Deven claimed as his own, always settling in and then pulling my arms around him—a cross between a chair and a hug. Darren turns from his comfortable position to face me and pronounces a bit challengingly, "This is mine now."

Then, as if he has second thoughts about making such a bold claim, he double-checks, "Okay?"

"It's yours, pal," I assure him. He sighs and settles in. Thank God, he doesn't ask me to embrace him. I am so hot.

We begin to share our memories of Deven, laughing at Jade's litany of his favorite cartoon and videos and how he could watch them over and over, perfectly memorized without ever missing a beat. Then his absolutely dapper taste in clothes and his nickname "Devonaire." Darren leaps up and imitates Deven strutting his stuff. We all laugh at memories of the twins as babies—Darren so laid back, Deven so intense, so ready to fly off the handle. How it took Darren so long to realize that during Deven's tantrums—in which he was often the victim of slapping hands, kicking feet, having his beloved pacifier knocked out of his mouth—that all he had to do was get out of the way. Brian and Jade imitate Darren's totally bewildered look during these times, and he cracks up.

Silence takes over. Jade suggests we sing a song—Deven's favorite.

Jesus loves me! This I know,
For the Bible tells me so.

Little ones to Him belong;
They are weak, but He is strong.
Yes, Jesus loves me.
Yes, Jesus loves me.
Yes, Jesus loves me.
The Bible tells me so.

There is no choice—either choke up or sing your heart out. We are loud, uneven, but sincere, with Raina's exquisite voice to guide us through and the children's absolute comfort at singing hymns in public.

Several moments after we finish, Raina announces, "Now I am going to sing it the way I used to do it for him when he was in bed with me, in the middle of the night."

On its own, her voice tells the whole story. It is almost a totally different song from the one just sang. She slows it way down, each syllable its own special moment, its own prayer. We bow our heads as Raina sings. But she does more than sing—she ministers to us as she ministered to him. I can see her with Deven, desperately ill, unable to sleep, in pain. I'm not sure when I've heard anything more beautiful. The song is a prayer—once such an empty aspect of my life, but always a full rich part of hers. I don't know how, but once again I feel the contradiction between deep sorrow, with streaks of unbelievable joy, and gratitude. I don't understand it. Now is not the time to figure it out. The word that keeps coming to me is "grace."

After a minute of quiet, Darren announces solemnly, "I wish we could dig him up."

It's one of those moments where adults silently communicate out of the corner of their eyes, *Oh God, I can't believe he just said that.* Along with, *No way am I touching that.*

Undeterred by the frozen, frightened silence, he suggests, "We could open up the box."

Jade has had just about enough. "Darren, *he's just bones.*"

Brian legitimizes the question, while clearly hoping he is not looking for trouble. "Darren, why do you want to do that?"

Without hesitation, he answers, "I want to make sure he's okay. And . . . and . . ." He looks like he's waiting for permission to continue.

He scans the circle—his beloved Mom holding Josiah, the baby brother Deven passed in transit; big sister, Jade; cousin Jah Nel; Aunt Martha; and Uncle Brian. A welcome breeze tickles the trees surrounding the cemetery, releasing a flock of swallows and momentarily blessing us with relief.

"And I would tell him . . . not to worry," Darren continues confidently, " 'cuz I think we're okay, too."

Acknowledgments

My editor Nancy Miller has been unfailingly generous with her skill, her encouragement, and her contagious enthusiasm for this book. I have thoroughly enjoyed working with her and look forward to future projects together. Her assistant Caroline Miller has greased all the necessary wheels with calm efficiency and kindness. Martha Schwartz and Laura Goldin gave my manuscript great care. Arielle Eckstut, my literary agent at Levine-Greenberg, remains a trusted advisor whose vision and friendship I appreciate beyond measure.

Raina gave me one of the greatest gifts of my life when she opened her door and allowed me to become part of her life, and gave me the chance to have a beautiful, funny, fulfilling roller coaster of a friendship.

I miss Deven every single day, but thank God for his sweet, boisterous, and joyous presence in our lives. His brothers Darren and Josiah, and sister Jade remind me to savor each moment we are given. In their increased regular contact with one another, may Jade, Darren, and their dad each feel more blessed.

My sister Sarah Manning and brother-in-law Scott Wilson have been generous beyond my wildest expectations and I will be grateful always. My parents John and Mary Louise Manning; my sisters Priscilla Ford and Rachel and her husband, Greg Hymel; and my brothers Mark and Chip Manning and his wife, Ann Simonini, are a constant source of love, support, and rich stories in the form of greatly inflated memories. No one makes me laugh so hard. Their openness to Raina and her kids was a gift to me as well.

John and Mary Depenbrock, David Cooney, Sallie Mink, Andrew Solomon, Ginger Hays, Pat Dalton, and Laura Galinson seemed to come through at just the right times.

Keara Manning Depenbrock has become a trusted sounding board for my writing and a constant source of surprise and joy. She may be an only child, but in my estimation, she's worth ten. Brian Depenbrock, husband and partner in this story, always knows whether I need a ready ear, a shoulder to cry on, or a swift kick in the ass. We have been together for thirty-four years and I love and thank him like crazy.

Jeremy Waletzky has for years been a trusted friend and guide through a breathless and sometimes treacherous rocky terrain. I am grateful for his wisdom, his constancy, and his gentle care. This book would not have been possible without him.